MONEY
LOVE
and
BITCOIN

Creating a Path to a Freer, Fairer,
and More Peaceful World

MONEY

LOVE

and

BITCOIN

PAUL J. ROGERS

BITS OF WISDOM *Press*

MONEY, LOVE, AND BITCOIN

Published by Bits of Wisdom Press
5342 Clark Rd. Suite 41108
Sarasota, FL 34233

ISBNs:
Paperback 979-8-9921147-0-6
eBook 979-8-9921147-1-3
Hardcover 979-8-9921147-2-0
Hardcover with Dust Jacket 979-8-9921147-3-7

Library of Congress Control Number: 2024926260

This book is a work of nonfiction. Every effort has been made to ensure the accuracy and completeness of the information provided herein. However, the author and publisher assume no responsibility for errors, omissions, or inaccuracies. The advice and strategies contained in this book are intended for informational purposes only and may not be suitable for every situation. Readers should seek professional advice where appropriate.

First Edition: February, 2025

Book designed by Mark Karis

Printed by Amazon and IngramSpark in the United States and other countries.

FOR DENISE, MITCH, AND GRACE

May we all contribute to and live in a freer, fairer, more peaceful and loving world.

Contents

"There is no wealth but life."—JOHN RUSKIN

Foreword

IT IS WITH GREAT PLEASURE that I recommend Paul Rogers's profound and timely book, *Money, Love, and Bitcoin: Creating a Path to a Freer, Fairer, and More Peaceful World*. Paul is a master teacher who has spent many years delving into personal growth and meditation. His deep commitment to conscious living and his sincere aspiration to bring more awareness into the financial realm is both inspiring and essential.

With an extensive background in finance and investment, Paul brings a unique blend of expertise to his work. His experience is complemented by his profound dedication to spiritual growth, having trained at Sattva Yoga Academy in the Himalayas, where he cultivated the ability to bridge the worlds of quantum mechanics, Eastern wisdom traditions, and financial acumen.

In *Money, Love, and Bitcoin*, Paul introduces a compelling vision of how we can integrate spiritual principles—such as energy, integrity, and love—into the world of finance. His work is a call to harmonize our monetary systems with higher values of unity and fairness, something that is urgently needed in today's world. Paul's insights into Bitcoin and the broader financial landscape are not just technical but deeply human and spiritual, pointing the way to a future where our financial systems are grounded in consciousness and compassion.

I highly recommend this book to anyone seeking not just a new perspective on money but a new way of being in the world—one where love and integrity guide our economic choices, creating a more peaceful and equitable future for all.

—**ANAND MEHROTRA,** ENTREPRENEUR, AUTHOR, AND FOUNDER OF SATTVA YOGA ACADEMY

Introduction

MONEY PLAYS A PIVOTAL ROLE in shaping the course of our lives and the world at large. It is a common thread woven into the fabric of nearly everything we do. The narrative of much of our existence revolves around the pursuit of money and financial stability to sustain ourselves and our families.

Although money infiltrates nearly every aspect of our lives, we seldom question the monetary system we are a part of or its fundamental structures. Our familiarity with the financial paradigms we have constructed has bred a sense of normalcy despite growing financial inequity, a consistent stream of economic crises, enormous debt burdens, and increasing polarization of opinions about what to do about these problems.

As cracks appear in our monetary structures and our society faces increasing divisions, it's crucial to comprehend the challenges we face and explore potential solutions. To do so, we must delve into the lifeblood of a fundamental societal mechanism—money. We must recognize the urgent need to scrutinize the very foundations of our global financial and monetary system. By understanding its intricate dynamics, we can gain insights into the issues that plague us and uncover avenues for positive change.

Having once navigated the world of investing as a financial advisor, I believed I had a solid grasp on the workings of money. While I was well-versed in the intricacies of the investment landscape, I had never delved deeply into understanding the true essence of money or how the distorted systems we've all grown accustomed to impact all aspects of our lives.

Throughout my twenty years in personal financial planning and investment management, I counseled hardworking people to save and invest so that they "wouldn't run out of money before they ran out of life." I was a Certified Financial Planner® and owned my own financial advisory and wealth management practice. Over the years, it became clear that many people were caught in the trap of thinking that saving and investing was just about the money and not about the life they wanted to lead using money as a tool. I also became a certified retirement coach to help people transition into the next stage of life with meaning and purpose. What I didn't realize at the time was how our flawed monetary system impacted everything I was trying to do to help my clients achieve their goals.

Many years ago, I faced the collapse of the life I had constructed based on following the usual program—go to school, get a job, get married, have kids, and live happily ever after. It's not a bad program, but the last part doesn't always work out that way. Out of the ashes, I met my now wife and number one supporter, Denise. She opened my mind and heart, inspiring me to return to the deeper questions I'd explored as a philosophy major in college, which had been calling me more and more. I started to follow her hand in hand, studying wisdom traditions from around the world, as well as investigating the principles upon which healthy communities and intimate relationships are built.

My financial advisory practice was successful, but these shifts made me realize that something else was calling me. While I loved my clients and truly enjoyed working with them, it was time to move on to something more personally fulfilling. I wasn't sure exactly what that would be, but I knew it would reveal itself once I put myself in a position to be open to new possibilities. This led me to sell my practice and begin the next stage of my evolutionary journey.

In March 2020, I went to Rishikesh, India, often called the "birthplace of yoga," for a long-postponed yoga training with a teacher my wife and I had been studying with for several years. While I was there, COVID-19 broke out, lockdowns started, and the world was turned upside down. I didn't immediately realize or understand how much this would impact Denise, me, and the world.

As an investment guy, it was obvious to me that the economy could not be shut down, and interest rates dropped to zero without having a significant impact. The US and most global stock markets initially plummeted but recovered quickly as the government began to inject massive amounts of money into the economy to replace the productivity lost when businesses were shuttered. It's common sense that if the economy is shut down, people can't work, and corporate earnings go down, stock markets should also. But what once was common sense no longer seemed to make sense. When the economy and markets shifted from real productivity to living on the flood of money pouring out of the government, we entered a new stage in a game that had been unfolding for the last few decades. Over time, it became more and more apparent that all the foundational investing principles I had learned and practiced were becoming irrelevant.

My aha moment came after seeing the "value" of our house rise nearly 25 percent in the one year since we bought it. While economists talk about the rate of inflation being a few percent, I realized that if we were buying our house at that point, it would have cost us 25 percent more than what we paid for it just a year earlier. This means that our inflation rate for purchasing a home was in the double digits. Cash sitting in the bank would have bought us 25 percent less house! It dawned on me that it wasn't that the "value" of our home was going up—it was that the value of what I was buying it with (US dollars) was *going down*. And that's what led me to dig deeper into what was really happening in our monetary system.

I used to dismiss the ominous warnings from "gold bugs," the fervent critics of the Federal Reserve System, and those advocating for alternative, seemingly archaic barter systems. In my perception, I resided in the "real world." Although I wasn't entirely content with what I observed, I failed to fathom the depth of the issues at hand or to explore any credible alternatives. That is, until now.

When this realization dawned on me, it led me to unravel the mechanisms of our monetary systems and unveil potential alternatives. This paradigm shift transformed my understanding and prompted me to reevaluate the economic and societal structures we often take for granted. What became clear to me were the distortions and dysfunctions in our current monetary system and the price we all pay for them. In other words, I realized that we need a new system.

As I searched for answers, I never imagined that I'd find something that at first seemed crazy, yet which I would end up believing holds the potential for transforming our monetary system and, therefore, our world. Though initially skeptical, I started researching Bitcoin and reading everything I could about it. This led me deep down the proverbial "Bitcoin rabbit hole." I came to understand what no one in the world of investment management ever taught me or discussed—what money really is and how our monetary system actually works. Once I discovered (rather than dismissed) Bitcoin, I began to see how it held the potential to address many of the problems inherent in our current systems. Despite all the answers I was finding, I still felt that something deeper needed to be understood and expressed about Bitcoin's importance.

Bitcoin is often perceived solely through the prism of currency, transactions, and our financial structures. However, beneath the surface lies a trove of fundamental principles whose pertinence extends beyond the confines of money and economics—principles that are often overlooked in the broader discourse. My desire in writing this book was to put together the pieces of a bigger puzzle.

Money, Love, and Bitcoin does not go into significant detail on monetary history and economic theory. You won't find it filled with charts and graphs or reams of economic data. Nor does it discuss Bitcoin's history at length, its technical operation, the cryptographic structures on which it is based, or the nuances of Bitcoin's protocols. There's a wealth of fantastic books, courses, and other resources available on these topics, and some are included in the "Resources and References" section of this book. (There, you will also find the link to a YouTube series I created under the moniker "Bits of Wisdom," which are ten short videos to help explain Bitcoin to friends and family.)

My principal aim for this book is to show that if we are to develop a better monetary system, it must be based on a universal foundation and framework and principles that transcend monetary theory. This new system must also be part of the broader development of new approaches and structures to support all of humanity. While this will take the work of thought leaders in economics, monetary systems, and technology, it will also take input from teachers on moral and ethical principles. These new systems and structures must be grounded in history and science as well as the more profound spiritual understanding that, while we are each a unique and sovereign individual, we live in an interconnected web of life.

Only with such a solid foundation will a new system be able to convince and attract enough people and have an enduring universal framework to make it viable and achieve its true potential. Together, we can guide the development and implementation of new systems on which to build a more just, compassionate, free, and self-sovereign system while recognizing the interdependent nature of all life.

In this book, I discuss the basics of money, how it works, and Bitcoin. What's crucial is that we understand what money truly is and that we take a step back to grasp how our current monetary system works. As you do, you'll see the problems our government-controlled system has caused. I also discuss the ramifications of our current system on everything from architecture to relationships and even sex.

If you're new to Bitcoin, I want to show you that it's about more than just money or technology. I've kept to the basics in this book, so you don't need to be a cryptography or financial expert to get why Bitcoin matters. Common sense will serve you quite well as you read it.

Finally, I delve into how a new monetary system and technological developments could lead to a freer, fairer, and more peaceful world. My goal is to help shed light on these matters without resorting to obtuse and obscure economic and financial jargon. Throughout the book, I also share teachings from various wisdom traditions on consciousness and our place in the universe to provide an alternate view of money and life. While the chapters build on each other, in many ways, each is a short essay highlighting a particular aspect of *Money, Love, and Bitcoin*.

If you're diving into this book without a clear grasp of what Bitcoin is, I aim to kick-start your exploration. For those already familiar with the monetary system and Bitcoin, I hope my point of view about it will be enlightening. If you've already done your research and understand Bitcoin, you may have thoroughly embraced the principles of a Bitcoin standard (a term made famous by Saifedean Ammous in his seminal work on Bitcoin titled *The Bitcoin Standard*.) This would mean that you value a permissionless, immutable, decentralized, open network supported by true proof of work and understand that trust should be held not in a central authority but in the protocol upon which a system is designed. It could also mean that you might be attracted to a more self-sovereign and autonomous system.

But you might not have gone even deeper and asked why the principles on which Bitcoin is based are critically important or how Bitcoin can connect to the greatest force in the universe. Bitcoin is often referred to as "freedom money." While it is described as a system free from control structures, what Bitcoin offers humanity the freedom *to do* is just as important.

In his book *The Fourth Turning Is Here*, Neil Howe suggests that we are at a point in regular historical cycles where old systems collapse and new ones are born. The tremendous pace of current technological advancements will shape a new world, though it may be hard to imagine the result. Transition periods are difficult and often lead to conflicting ideas about how new systems should be designed. R. Buckminster Fuller recommends, "You never change things by fighting the existing reality. To change something, build a new model that makes the existing model obsolete." The essence of this book is to describe the pathway and principles of how to do just that. The answer lies in love.

So here you are at the end of a long introduction and probably asking the question Tina Turner sang about in her hit song, "What's Love Got to Do with It." Read on, and I'll walk you through it so you can come to your own conclusion. Then, hopefully, we can journey together on the path to creating a freer, fairer, more loving and peaceful world.

1

What is Money?

The people must be helped to think naturally about money. They must be told what it is, and what makes it money, and what are the possible tricks of the present system which put nations and peoples under control of the few.

—HENRY FORD

BEING INSPIRED BY THE WORDS OF MR. FORD set me up for a big task, but it's the right one. More than a century ago, this industrial leader recognized the need for education about our monetary system and its manipulations. It's fair to say we've drifted even further from understanding the true nature of money since then. Governments, economists, and financial institutions have clouded our natural understanding with complex terms, fancy financial products, and mysterious jargon. Central bankers and economists share their ideas from ivory towers, flipping common sense upside down. Meanwhile, those pulling the strings and playing "tricks" amass more power and wealth, tightening their grip on nations and people.

To grasp what's truly unfolding in our economies and monetary systems, let's step back from our bank accounts, cash in wallets, and credit cards—things we commonly think of as money. We must question what we think we know about money, scrutinize the information we receive, and figure out who benefits from the existing monetary structures. Let's dig into what money represents, why we have the national currencies we do, and the problems of a government-controlled monetary system. Understanding these elements is crucial to recognizing the pros and cons of this system and exploring potential solutions. The good news? It's not as complicated as the system makes it seem.

THE FUNCTIONS OF MONEY

Money has three functions: a unit of account, a medium of exchange, and a store of value. A unit of account means each unit has the same value, so units can be counted and used to assess relative value. Anything that can be divided into units and counted would work as long as everyone agrees, making it a common currency. It's a lot easier to use a standard unit to account for value than trying to figure out in myriad transactions how much of one thing should be exchanged for another (e.g., how many potatoes should be of equal value to a cow). Historically, units were some material objects (seashells, glass beads, precious items, or gold and silver). This is referred to as "commodity money."

A second key feature of money is that it is a medium of exchange. Whether it is digging rocks out of the ground, growing vegetables, providing medical advice, creating art, engineering a bridge, or building a house, all these expenditures of energy have value. When the goods and services produced from these efforts are seen as valuable by other members of society, we can exchange them with others for products we need. In a simple economy, barter may be adequate for this exchange. However, when economies expand and labor becomes more specialized, barter becomes inefficient as it is unlikely that whom you want to barter with wants what you have produced or that there is proportional value. For example, bartering eggs for building a house isn't going to work. The builder could never use that many eggs, nor do they want to be in the business of further bartering eggs for the things they do need.

Instead, money is a technological convenience for the exchange of value or energy. When we use a shared money system, we can know how many units of something we must accumulate to buy something we want, for example, the number of apples we would have to grow to buy a dress. Common money can serve as an effective medium of exchange by making transactions easy and convenient. We can just use monetary units in transactions rather than bartering.

The third function of money is to store any excess earned from our labor to buy goods in the future, to provide a safety net during hard times, to pass on to our children, or to invest in the activities of others in the hope of increasing our capital. Money that acts as an effective store of value is called sound or hard money, usually because it is backed by some scarce commodity, historically gold or silver. Easy money or fiat (meaning created or decreed by authority) currency refers to units that are not backed by a scarce commodity but rather are paper units easily created by governments and central banks. There is little cost to making more paper money, so its supply tends to expand.

In summary, money is simply a derivative technology used to store, account for, and exchange value/energy between people. Throughout history, people have used various things to serve the purpose of money's technology. It is essential to have a foundational understanding of what money is and what systems have been used to represent it if we are to understand their strengths and weaknesses and consider other technologies.

In most "developed" countries, money has worked smoothly for engaging in and keeping accounts of transactions. But it's a different story in many parts of the world—especially the Global South. There, people struggle with expensive or hard-to-reach banking and financial systems, making monetary transactions a real challenge. In fourteen countries in Africa, the only legal currency, the Central African franc, is an enduring and, some say, an enslaving and exploitative vestige of the French colonial empire. In countries worldwide, in the name of wars or anti-terrorism efforts or to control the money flow, governments put a squeeze on people's ability to carry out transactions freely.

The three functions of money are increasingly breaking down, to varying degrees, throughout the world. Under our current systems, money is subject to manipulation and distortion, which undermines our money's ability to act as an effective means of trade or store of value.

AN ALTERNATIVE VIEW OF MONEY

Whether you study quantum physics or ancient spiritual traditions (or both), they tell the same tale: Everything is energy.

Energy condenses into material phenomena that we perceive with our human senses. While form is real in terms of how we operate in the everyday material world, at another level, it is an illusion because, underneath the layer of base perception, all is energy.

So, what is energy? Energy is the vibrational field that underlies and connects all that is. It expresses itself in frequencies or vibrational waves. Due to the limitations of our five senses, we don't perceive these frequencies directly. We can only interpret their effects. We cannot see light frequencies, but our brains interpret how these frequencies bounce off matter to tell us what we are looking at. Our ears translate another type of invisible frequency into nerve signals, which the brain experiences as sound. Some are long waves, and some are short. Some are audible to humans, others to dogs.

We cannot discern different frequencies by looking at the air through which they travel, nor can we see how some may be blocked by walls, some limited by distance, and others may be jammed. Perceiving a transmission and its message depends on whether we have the right receiver (our ears or bodies, a radio, TV, or cell phone). All of these frequences or waves are energy forms operating within a field.

The same is true for money; it is a frequency. Just as a wave in an ocean is an aspect of the ocean, while at the same time not separate from it, money is simply a part or expression of a larger form of energy. If we think of money as some separate and distinct material form, we fail to understand it.

Let's discuss what the energy of money really is. It's a signal between people who are generators and transmitters of energy. We generate or transform life and material energy into labor, goods, and services and convert that into a signal—money—that can be transmitted and shared. We are the generators of what

13

money represents—not any government! Only through creativity, hard work, ingenuity, and the expression of our innate gifts and talents can we create the value that money represents. Author and leadership expert Robin Sharma said, "Money is nothing more than a reflection of your creativity, your capacity to focus, and your ability to add value and receive back."

Money is an energetic frequency much like any other; it's like a sound wave in the form of a radio transmission. If you have a receiver, such as a radio, you can tune in to the frequency, hear the signal, and receive the sound. As we have voices that can generate and transmit sound, we also have ears that receive the signal and a brain that processes the signal into meaning. Money is like a sound wave being transmitted between people. Money, like sound, carries messages. A monetary system with integrity uses money to convey the message of how much work someone has done to earn and accumulate it.

Just as modern physics shows us that everything is energy, systems theory in biology and ecology demonstrates that all life on earth is an interconnected web. We breathe in oxygen and exhale carbon dioxide. Trees breathe in carbon dioxide and exhale oxygen. Nothing is a stand-alone, self-contained unit. Material form reduces to atoms, but an atom is composed of energy "packets" in relative positions to other energy packets, all of which are influenced by the perspective and perception of the human observer. Modern physics teaches that everything in the universe is connected and all form arises from an underlying field of "nothingness."

Similarly, the great wisdom traditions also teach that everything is connected, arises from a single source, and is a product of that source. All material forms emerge from the underlying formless nature of pure being. We are all part of this consciousness, this energy, this light, this love. However, the source of this energy is not the nation-state, and neither is it the source of authentic money.

NATION-STATE MONEY

A wholly new monetary experiment was initiated when money was divorced from an underlying scarce material good and replaced solely with state-created paper notes. In the last hundred years or so, the idea of money as something that is manufactured, managed, and legally approved by a nation has gained predominance. It's all most of us have ever known, so it seems normal, but it is anything but normal in human history.

Let's pick up the radio analogy again. What if every signal—every voice—was required to transmit at only the frequency authorized by a central authority? And what if that central authority was the only one that could create the frequency for transmitting messages from one party to others? Suppose there was a separate central authority in each country on earth, and they all used different transmission wavelengths within their borders. This would require special decoders to convert the frequency of one country's signal into another's so that people in other countries could understand the transmitted messages, wouldn't it? It's not hard to imagine that some central authorities might have stronger transmitters that could drown out the signals of others. Or that some countries could project their signals so loudly and strongly that they become the dominant signals heard around the world. What would happen if one nation that didn't like another nation jammed its signal and prevented the flow of its wavelengths to other parties?

This is, in essence, our fiat monetary system. Legal currencies are only created by nation-states and generally cannot be used across borders. That is unless, like the United States, the transmitter of the signal (the dollar) is so powerful it blasts the sound so loudly that other signals become staticky and lose clarity. One of the reasons the United States can project its signal worldwide is because it has transmitters, the US armed forces, located around the world. Because the United States can project power globally through its military might, it can transmit its signal more powerfully than most other countries. Every warship, every military base, and every missile is basically a repeater transmitter sending and enforcing the signals sent from Washington, DC.

When one country has a dominant global economic and military presence, its money can act as a "global reserve currency." A reserve currency is essentially such a super strong signal that much of the world ends up using and listening only to that channel. It becomes the dominant message, and all the weaker signals get lost. Most importantly, when a nation has that strong of a signal, it gets to broadcast whatever it wants, whether it is real, true, or of underlying value. It also spreads the cost of its profligacy around the world because people outside its borders use its devaluing currency.

CORRUPTED MONEY

Money is simply a technology for exchanging energy between humans. But corrupted exchange technologies, like disrupted sound or light frequencies, distort the pure transfer of money's energy. Furthermore, physics' law of the conservation of energy holds that energy can neither be created nor destroyed. This means that the government cannot create energy (true money) out of nothing simply by running the printing presses or adding digits to accounts.

Instead, what happens is that the energetic signals transmitted in the form of money get diluted. Just as when a scientist adds more water to a solution, the substance or solute in it becomes diluted, the energy of money gets diluted when the government creates fiat money without any actual energy input created by human work. Real money energy is a reflection of proof of work. "Proof of work" is a term used to mean that real-life force or energy is expended in the process of creating something. It's not a matter of what you own or how powerful you are. It's a matter of what you do. Energy and love are abundant and infinite, but their source is not politicians or governments.

A big problem arises when people think the government is the source of money. When the government is seen as the creator and distributor of money, and crony capitalism results in those closest to the government getting most of it, a feeling of inequity arises. Bankers get bailed out, but families struggling to keep their homes do not.

This leads to the belief that the system is rigged against ordinary people, so why bother? Why shouldn't we just demand that the government hand over the money to us, instead of us having to create value and earn it? If others are going to siphon off the system, why not everyone? When fewer and fewer people are adding value, the entire system becomes a debt-fueled frenzy, leading to moral and financial bankruptcy.

2

Why is There Inflation?

Inflation is always and everywhere a monetary phenomenon in the sense that it is and can be produced only by a more rapid increase in the quantity of money than in output.
— MILTON FRIEDMAN

ONE OF THE WORST OUTCOMES of the corruption of money is the inherent inflation built into government money. We've been duped into thinking that inflation is just some natural law of economics, but it is not. It is a symptom of a distorted debt-based system that requires the systematic devaluation of money. (I talk more about this in chapter 7.)

So, let's peel the onion back to try to really grasp what

inflation is and why it happens. I'm going to try to keep this simple to illustrate the primary factors. Prices are generally determined by supply and demand. If there is more demand for something than there is supply, prices rise. Similarly, prices fall when there is a plentiful supply of something but demand is stable or declining. When prices rise (more demand), producers produce more, and when prices fall (less demand), they produce less. As the factors causing something's supply and demand change, prices rise and fall in response.

THE MONEY SUPPLY

What most people don't understand is that the money supply rises and falls based on the actions of governments and central banks. They adjust and manipulate the supply of money to influence economic decisions. An easy example is to look at interest rates. Low interest rates encourage people to take out loans and buy things. High interest rates discourage borrowing. Without government and central bank involvement, the market would set interest rates based on market participants' assessment of various factors. For example, the riskier a borrower is, the higher the interest rate they will have to pay. That's easy to understand. However, when central banks determine interest rates, market forces become less relevant, and the policy decisions and biases of unelected committees become the primary factors. The forces and intent behind these decisions are often opaque and obfuscated. The former chair of the US Federal Reserve, Alan Greenspan, who made a career and an art of ensuring that what he said was confusing and ambiguous, once said, "I guess I should warn you, if I turn out to be particularly clear, you've probably misunderstood what I said."

These less transparent factors, not market forces, contribute to both systemically rising prices and spikes in inflation. Let's use an example of an apple farmer to illustrate how normal price movements work so we can contrast it with non-market-based interference. If a farmer produces one hundred bushels of apples and takes them to the market, they may be worth enough for him to buy ten chickens. Now, if there is a bad harvest, fewer apples will be available, but if people still want them, then the price of apples will rise, so maybe the farmer will get twelve chickens for one hundred bushels of apples. Similarly, if the apple crop is huge one year, prices will likely fall because there is more supply compared to demand. These are normal, unmanipulated market forces at work.

Now, consider the scenario where someone arrives in town with a truckload of new apples. This increase in the apple supply will likely lead to a decrease in prices. In the conventional world, bringing apples to the market entails significant effort and investment, including the acquisition of land for planting, the meticulous care and cultivation of apple trees, and the timely harvesting of the fruit. To yield a large quantity of apples, tangible and substantial work involving a considerable amount of energy is required (demonstrable proof of work).

A farmer decides to invest time, resources, and labor in producing more apples only if they believe the apples' selling price will exceed the production cost. In this way, the dynamics of supply, demand, and production costs interplay to determine the feasibility of such an investment for the farmer.

Suppose a farmer could create apples with no investment and no need to buy land, plant trees, or harvest and transport the fruit. Impossible, you say. Yes, it would be. In the "real" economy, effort is required to produce goods. But all this gets turned upside down when it comes to "producing" currency.

In a system with integrity, a government could only spend money from the taxes it collects from people doing actual work in the real economy. But in a fiat monetary system, governments can create money at the press of a button. The currency isn't supported by real work. Neither the government nor its citizens produced more apples for the money created!

When the government increases the supply of money just by printing it, the value of what is created—money—falls. It's like if our magic apple producer arrives in town with a truck full of apples that they dump at the market; the real farmer will see the value of apples fall if demand remains unchanged. So, when more units of paper money are produced without any actual economic value added to the system, the units are worth less.

Let's continue with the example of the apples but in a broader, though admittedly simplified, illustration. If there are one hundred dollars in a system and one hundred apples, each apple would be worth one dollar. If there are only fifty apples, each would be worth two dollars. Suppose an extra hundred dollars is added to the system, but there are still only one hundred apples; now, each apple is "worth" two dollars. Here, it isn't the supply of apples that changed but the supply of money! It's not that the apples are worth more; it's that the currency is diluted and so worth less. The price of apples has been inflated for reasons unrelated to normal market forces.

THE TWO SIDES OF INFLATION

The Roman god Janus is depicted as having two faces looking in opposite directions, one forward and one backward. The term "Janus-faced" means someone or something that exhibits two contrasting aspects; it also means being duplicitous or deceitful. Inflation is like this. We see one face—rising prices of goods and services extending forward into the future. But, the other face is the falling currency value due to the past actions of governments influencing the money supply. They are two aspects of the same coin. The duplicity comes when our system's money masters only point to one side of the coin. Inflation is blamed on external forces that must be managed and subdued by central banks. Yet, this is a deceitful presentation. We must also look at the other side of the coin, backward at the inflationary actions of the government and central bank that increased the money supply and thereby decreased its value.

When governments flood economies with units of currency created out of thin air, prices rise. Did the value of apples really go up, or did the value of what you are buying them with decline? Remember my aha moment, mentioned in the introduction, after the government flooded the economy with more money during COVID-19?

We have come to believe that inflation is a normal part of any economic system. In truth, it is not. Rather, it is the effect of a monetary system that is distorted away from what is normal— the actual value of energy as denominated in units of currency. In a true free market, prices will fall as people become more efficient and productive in producing goods and services. With all the incredible technological and productivity improvements we've seen in the recent past, prices should actually be falling. If not for the dilution in currency values by governments making more of it, prices would be falling, and life would be getting easier, not harder!

In the United States, the Federal Reserve has normalized a target inflation rate of 2 percent as a beneficial standard. What if that was rephrased to, "Our target is to cut the value of your labor and savings in half every thirty-six years"? It's the same damn thing! That's the math. Oh, and by the way, the value of your money is being debased much faster than that! On top of that, when you consider that prices should be falling, the real inflation rate is substantially larger. This is a theft of the value of our work resulting from a debt-based, centrally controlled system used to benefit those in power.

The consumer price index (CPI) in the United States (and its corollaries in other countries) is the metric used to measure the rate of inflation. The government determines and collects the data to generate the index. And it is the government that decides to change how the data is measured to serve its political interests and/or mask the real impacts of its actions.

As an example, in the United States, when the prices of higher value goods increase (which would cause the inflation rate to increase), the methodology is to replace the higher quality/higher priced goods in the index with lower quality (and therefore lower priced) goods, which prevents the index from rising by the true measure of price increases. For example, suppose the price of sirloin steak increases; the index assumes consumers will switch to lower-priced ground beef, so the actual increase in the cost of meat is not accurately measured. It's a shell game that manipulates the CPI and hides the real impact of currency devaluation. It is a fraud and crime against the citizenry. However, this war against the populace's purchasing power is not the only conflict engendered by a corrupted monetary system (as discussed in chapter 4). In the face of rising prices that result from increasing the money supply, how do people preserve the value of their work and savings? Let's turn to that next.

3

The Attraction of Money

The force of gravity is the force of attraction between all masses in the universe; it pulls things toward each other.

— STEPHEN HAWKING

IN PHYSICS, the strength of gravity's pull is determined by the mass of the objects involved. Those with a larger mass exert a greater gravitational force. Similarly, money's strength is based on the amount of energy it attracts and stores—its "mass." Gold, as a technology of money, has attracted energy and had great gravitational pull as a store of wealth for centuries.

In today's world, we primarily use paper notes (or their

digital equivalent) denominated in a country's currency to store the energy of our labor. Some currencies are chosen as money for trade or storage much more than others because these national currencies are more attractive than those of other countries. The total amount of wealth stored in United States dollars, euros, or Chinese yuan is orders of magnitude larger than that stored in the Zimbabwean dollar or the Laotian kip.

This is a function of both the size of a nation's economy as well as its ability to attract energy from economic activity outside its borders, which, together, reflects the currency's "mass" and, therefore, its "gravitational pull." The more a form of money attracts us to use it, the more potent and influential its "signal" or pull becomes. Similarly, the less appealing a currency is as a form of money, the more other assets are used to store value.

A MONEY BATTERY

If we want to store some of the energy of our life's labor, we need something to hold it. This is either currency or some other storage device. Let's use the analogy of a battery to illustrate the next point. A battery is a useful way to store electrical energy. Any battery that is better at storing and preserving energy will, in time, be the one people want, for example, lithium versus alkaline batteries. Even so, if most electrical devices only use a less efficient battery, it will take time for a more efficient or better battery to attract the development of more devices that use the better battery.

Fiat currency operates much like entropy, displaying a tendency to lose information in transmission and revert to a state of disorder. While this is not an inherent trait of a fiat, government-controlled currency, it becomes one due to human behavior, politics, and government agendas. Thus, entropy might as well be considered a thermodynamic law of government money because such a system consistently, and at times dramatically, dilutes stored value, rendering it worth less, just like a battery loses charge. The energy wasn't expended. The storage unit just wasted it. The currency isn't the actual value of productive effort's energy; it's merely a more or less efficient technology for storing or transferring it.

Consider a scenario where a battery is designed and advertised to intentionally lose energy at the rate of at least 2 percent per year but actually loses energy at a 7 percent yearly rate. What if, at times, and when used in certain devices, its power depletes by 20 percent or more in a single year? Now, replace "a battery" in the first sentence with "the US dollar" and think of the energy loss percentages as discounts to the dollar's value. Those discounts (the energy losses) are even larger if the example is the currency of a nation subject to hyperinflation. In 2023, the rate of inflation of the Venezuelan bolivar was 210 percent, the Zimbabwean dollar 285 percent, and the Argentinean peso 73 percent. NATO-member Turkey's lira fell 72 percent. Keeping up with the magnitude of loss of purchasing power at these inflation rates through increased wages is impossible. The only solution is to get your savings out if you can.

While those in the United States are more fortunate, they do not escape the systemic decline in the purchasing power of the US dollar. For example, the stated inflation target of the US Federal Reserve is 2 percent, but the actual monetary inflation rate has been around 7 percent. During the COVID-19 pandemic, the United States created approximately 40 percent more units of dollar money than it had in its entire history. Initially, the money being distributed at that time may have seemed beneficial for the country. However, the new units rapidly devalued the stored energy in the dollar, and the consequences became evident when prices soared, requiring more money to purchase the same products due to the inflationary impact of the dilution.

Those in control, who benefit most from the system, offer various explanations for what's happening in such circumstances, deflecting blame from their own actions. Factors like supply chain or manufacturing disruptions indeed restrict the availability of goods and naturally can lead to price hikes, but more is going on. And, as I mentioned earlier, shouldn't productivity and technological improvements result in lower prices anyway?

WHERE ELSE CAN I STORE MY MONEY IF NOT IN MONEY?

When people see their savings storage devices lose energy, they look for other things to store their savings in. Imagine holding numerous batteries that are rapidly losing energy. The logical move would be to either 1) use up the energy quickly or 2) switch to alternative storage. With number one, when a currency behaves like a fast-depleting battery, people tend to spend it before its purchasing power diminishes. In Weimar Germany, for example, after the "war to end all wars," it took a wheelbarrow of paper money to buy a loaf of bread. No one held on to this money for the future. Those units were more valuable as fuel for heat than as storage for future purchases. Throughout history, failed currencies often follow this pattern, revealing the significant challenges brought on by skyrocketing inflation in countries with crumbling fiat currencies.

Alternatively, we can move to option two when existing batteries don't hold a charge. This is when people are compelled to find new ways to store energy, which is the shift we've seen over the last few decades—the monetization of alternative assets. Instead of storing value solely in currency, individuals now invest in stocks, bonds, real estate, art, collectibles, and more as their chosen repositories for energy. While this has been happening for some time, it was especially apparent after the Great Recession.

After the "Great Financial Crisis" in 2008–2009, the US Federal Reserve and numerous central banks deliberately suppressed market interest rates to spur consumption, further encouraging people to move from savings to other investments. When faced with the certainty of at least 2 percent inflation and earning 0 percent on savings, the incentive arises to borrow at low rates and either spend or "invest" existing funds before their value dwindles. And if you are a large financial institution close to the money printer, you get the benefit of accessing money at these low rates to buy other assets before any cash trickles down to others.

REAL ESTATE

During this period, the prevailing wisdom was to shift from cash to stocks, bonds, or real estate, guided by the notion (coincidentally) of TINA—There Is No Alternative. This shift elevates the relative prices of these assets because they become "monetized." Essentially, they assume a value beyond their intrinsic investment or utility, effectively being treated as a form of money.

Let's first look at residential real estate. Traditionally, houses were meant to be homes to live in, but they have been transformed into investments rather than dwelling places. Typically, the supply of building materials and labor, along with land-use restrictions, would affect the amount of new construction and, therefore, ultimately, real estate prices. However, a closer look at various markets reveals that's not the whole story. In reality, what we observe in the real estate market is an acceleration of a trend that has been unfolding over an extended period that is unrelated to traditional supply and demand issues.

Soaring prices, even for basic homes outside prime locations, reflect values beyond being family residences. It's an "investment" fueled by low interest rates and a debt-based system. For example, real estate brokerage firm Redfin reported that in the fourth quarter of 2021, investor purchases of single-family homes soared to a record high of 18.4 percent. A November 3, 2023, article, "How Institutional Buyers Are Changing the Face of the U.S. Housing Market," by Chris MacDonald on Yahoo!Finance reports:

> Following the 2008 foreclosure crisis, large institutional investors, backed by Wall Street capital, acquired hundreds of thousands of single-family homes, resulting in a significant growth of institutionally owned single-family rentals (SFRs). By 2019, these companies had amassed a portfolio of over 200,000 homes valued at more than $30 billion...
>
> The entry of institutional buyers into the single-family housing market quickly led to increased housing prices. Their substantial financial resources allowed them to outcompete individual buyers, causing prices to rise. That made it even harder for first-time homebuyers to afford homes in already challenging markets due to reduced inventory caused by institutional purchases.

The monetization of real estate has huge impacts on everyday working families. The rising unaffordability of homes means people are forced to spend more of their income on basic shelter.

A US Congressional Research Service report, "Housing Wealth and Homeownership Trends: Implications for Economic Mobility and Policy," from July 7, 2023, stated:

> Prices for both homeowners and renters have increased over recent decades, even when controlling for inflation and income. Rental and owned-housing affordability indexes have also shown a trend of decreasing affordability in the past decade, and cost burdens are fairly widespread for those at or below median income.

Anna Bahney reported, "Home Affordability Is the Worst It Has Been Since 1984," for CNN on August 24, 2023:

> Buying a house requires a much bigger slice of people's income now—making this the most unaffordable housing market since 1984 by one measure. And that crushing lack of affordability isn't expected to improve much in the near future. To put today's affordability levels in perspective, it would take some combination of up to a 28% decline in home prices, a more than 4% reduction in 30-year mortgage rates, or up to a 60% growth in median household incomes to bring home affordability back to its 25-year average," said Andy Walden, vice president of enterprise research and strategy at Black Knight.

Amid the rising unaffordability of homes and the stories, charts, and data illustrating the past affordability of homes on a single income, it's crucial to unravel the underlying reasons. While interest rates, supply, and restrictions on new home building affect prices, another factor is that the true value of real estate isn't necessarily rising; rather, what you're purchasing it with is losing value.

A three-bedroom home doesn't offer more utility as a living space now than it did fifty years ago. The battery meant to store energy from wages and savings is leaking its charge. The US dollar has lost about 99 percent of its purchasing power since 1913 (the year the Federal Reserve was created). If wages or one's share of increased economic productivity were rising proportionally, it might be less of an issue. Unfortunately, for many, wealth inequality is surging. According to a Pew Research Center report from January 9, 2020:

> A greater share of the nation's aggregate income is now going to upper-income households and the share going to middle- and lower-income households is falling. The share of American adults who live in middle-income households has decreased from 61% in 1971 to 51% in 2019. This downsizing has proceeded slowly but surely since 1971, with each decade thereafter typically ending with a smaller share of adults living in middle-income households than at the beginning of the decade.

Take note of this date of 1971 since, as we'll discuss shortly, a very significant event in monetary history happened then. Notably, the decline mentioned in the report predates the surge in government money printing and resulting inflation triggered by the COVID-19 pandemic.

STOCKS

When I had my financial advisory practice, many of my clients didn't really want to take on the risks associated with investing in stocks. They just knew there was little choice because they couldn't preserve their wealth by keeping it in the bank. Many of us have been forced to invest when all we want to do is save.

A whole discipline of "behavioral finance" emerged to explain people's reactions and behaviors when faced with the potential for gains versus the fear or reality of loss. Its main objective often involves convincing individuals to embrace discomfort for the sake of potential financial growth. However, from my experience, most people simply want to safeguard their savings. While growth is appealing, they aren't aspiring venture capitalists willing to risk everything for outsize returns.

The imperative to "invest" stems from an inflationary system that makes preserving purchasing power challenging without embracing higher risk. Consequently, many find themselves compelled to enter the market, often against their preferences. Even for those with sufficient resources and the time to comprehend market dynamics (or seek assistance), the volatility of markets can be incredibly unnerving. For individuals aiming to savor their retirement, the anxiety of potentially losing their nest egg in a market crash adds unwelcome stress. And, if you don't have the savings to even be in the market, you are moving your piece around the board as fast as you can but only going backward.

Companies' underlying, intrinsic values aren't the only influence on stock valuations; they're also affected by the perception that the stock market is a superior means of preserving purchasing power compared to bank savings. It's crucial to recognize that money directed out of cash and into stocks, bonds, or real estate influences the prices of these assets. This flight into the market drives up share prices.

FROM GOLD TO THE PETRODOLLAR

Gold served as money (or the backing for the government's paper money) for thousands of years. Gold was an effective form of sound money because of how difficult it is to expand its supply, given that it is limited in the earth's crust and costly to mine. Gold was also a good form of money because it is very durable and was broadly accepted. However, gold's role as a form of money declined due to its inefficiency in transferring value as trade expanded globally. Physically moving gold over long distances was costly and risky. This led to the creation of more efficient paper representations and ledger systems for gold. However, this relationship was severed when governments sought to break free from the constraints of gold-backed paper. The era of the United States' full-fledged fiat currency began only recently when, in 1971, President Richard Nixon "temporarily" suspended the conversion of paper dollars into gold. (We'll discuss that more in chapter 7.)

In the early 1970s, around the time when Nixon removed the United States from the gold standard, another significant global event unfolded. Amid geopolitical developments in the Middle East, oil-producing nations organized to exert pressure on the United States and other countries. The Organization of Petroleum Exporting Countries (OPEC) implemented oil embargoes, leading to surging prices and gasoline shortages.

Much like Shakespeare's notion that "misery acquaints a man with strange bedfellows," a unique situation emerged. In response to the crisis, oil-exporting countries agreed to price and sell oil in US dollars exclusively, forming what is known as the petrodollar system. Consequently, the US dollar became the essential currency for the global oil trade. Furthermore, the US military, albeit tacitly, assumed the role of securing global transport and shipping channels critical for the oil trade.

Coupled with its military might and economic dominance after World War II, the petrodollar arrangement further ensured that the US dollar was the dominant global currency because it meant most countries needed dollars to buy and sell oil. The US dollar became the most powerful attractor of energy and became the global reserve currency.

Being a reserve currency offers significant advantages but also entails crucial responsibilities. The stability and accessibility of the currency are paramount in maintaining its effectiveness in this role. However, when geopolitical considerations turn the currency into a tool for sanctions—restricting nations or entities from participating in global financial systems or freezing dollar accounts—distrust grows, and the currency's utility diminishes.

Recent global events have prompted some nations to reconsider the petrodollar arrangement. Both nations and individuals are exploring alternatives to the US dollar's role as the global reserve currency. The BRICS countries (named after Brazil, Russia, India, China, and South Africa, but now comprising many other nations) are organizing to consider alternatives to US dollar hegemony. Some are turning to other fiat currencies and arrangements, while others are increasingly focusing on the emerging technology of Bitcoin, which is gaining attention and momentum.

BITCOIN ENTERS THE EQUATION OF MONEY

Let's go back to our battery analogy. Imagine a battery with infinite capacity, a set limit on the total number of cells ever created, and the remarkable potential to preserve and conserve 100 percent of transferred energy. Picture a scenario where no single country or manufacturer controls its production, and every person worldwide can access such a battery using one of the most ubiquitous devices on the planet. What if the network of devices and individuals dedicated to using this battery is growing exponentially? Envision that the battery's power can be transferred anywhere on the globe, to anyone, 24/7/365, without hefty fees depleting the battery's energy. Well, that battery would be a winner, wouldn't it? This encapsulates the promise and potential of Bitcoin.

Michael Saylor, a graduate of the Massachusetts Institute of Technology with dual degrees in aeronautics and astronautics, as well as science, technology, and society, is the visionary leader of MicroStrategy, a business intelligence and enterprise software company. He made waves by adopting a groundbreaking corporate strategy—using Bitcoin as a treasury asset. The company bought Bitcoin instead of holding its excess profits in losing-value cash or US Treasuries. Since 2020 when he adopted this strategy, he has emerged as a prominent advocate and educator on the principles and technology behind Bitcoin. If you haven't delved into the plethora of speeches and interviews he has delivered, I highly recommend doing so. According to Saylor, "Bitcoin is the most efficient system in the history of mankind for channeling energy through time and space." If you want to channel the stored energy of your life's labor, don't you want to find the most efficient system for doing so?

Since its inception in 2008 with no initial energy or value,

Bitcoin's stored energy value has surged to well over a trillion dollars and is growing rapidly. Its increasing allure and the desire to shift from energy stored in fiat currencies to a more efficient battery are propelling the Bitcoin network into a global force.

As more energy gravitates toward Bitcoin, its price, when measured in other currency units, experiences upward momentum. The overarching trend over the last sixteen years is evident—compared to Bitcoin, fiat is depreciating (though the price of Bitcoin in fiat may exhibit notable fluctuations due to its status as an emerging technology). If you price goods in fiat currencies, prices are going up. If you price goods in Bitcoin, prices are going down!

A pivotal concept in computing and systems is the network effect. The network effect is the principle that the more people who use a particular network, the more valuable and widespread it becomes until its use becomes self-reinforcing and it prevails as the dominant network. When the TCP/IP and HTTP protocols governing the Internet were introduced, they were not the only options, yet because they achieved global user adoption, they became standards—a testament to the pervasive and powerful nature of the network effect.

Recent government action in the United States and elsewhere has provided regulatory clarity surrounding Bitcoin. Where once there was concern that the government would ban Bitcoin, with the launch of government-approved investing vehicles (exchange traded funds/products) in the United States, Canada, Germany, Australia, Hong Kong, and other countries, that ship has sailed. In just a few months after their launch, Bitcoin ETFs in the United States attracted capital from a wide swath of investment managers and pension funds. These ETFs have been the most successful ETF products launched (attracting the most money in the shortest period) in history.

While there are still Bitcoin opponents, the tide of legislative and regulatory action is turning, and it seems clear that Bitcoin is here to stay, and its acceptance will only expand. Legislation has been introduced in the United States Congress to establish a "strategic Bitcoin reserve" wherein the United States would buy one million Bitcoin over the next five years. It has also been suggested that the United States should sell some of its large gold reserves to purchase Bitcoin. Several states have legislation protecting the rights of Bitcoin holders, and some are also discussing purchasing it as a reserve asset. It is becoming clear that Bitcoin is being viewed by many as the potential new global foundation of sound money.

All this is on the heels of El Salvador adopting Bitcoin as legal tender in 2021. The global establishment roundly criticized the move when President Nayib Bukele adopted it and started buying Bitcoin as a reserve asset. On January 25, 2022, The Financial Times reported "The IMF has urged El Salvador to stop recognizing bitcoin as a legal tender in the country and expressed concern over its plan to issue bonds linked to the cryptocurrency." Yet on December 6, 2024, as Bitcoin crossed the $100,000 US dollar mark, AP News reported "El Salvador's president is triumphant after his bet on bitcoin comes true."

The adoption of a Bitcoin strategy along with a crackdown on gangs were fundamental components of Bukele's plan to transform his country of El Salvador from a "murder capital" to a safe, fiscally sound country with a renewed and energized entrepreneurial spirit. As World Briefings reported on September 25, 2024, "El Salvador's transformation under President Nayib Bukele has been nothing short of remarkable. Once one of the most dangerous countries in the world, El Salvador is now ranked as the 8th safest nation, according to recent reports." And as Bukele announced in a post on X on December 5, 2024, El Salvador is sitting on a 117 percent return or $300 million dollar gain on its Bitcoin holdings.

All this is creating more discussion and activity in countries across the world. The Street reported on November 13, 2024:

> The Bitcoin market is buzzing with rumors and speculations about nation-states accumulating BTC to strengthen their strategic reserves. From the U.S. to Middle Eastern countries, major players may be entering the crypto landscape in a big way, potentially fueling a Bitcoin supercycle… If the speculation around nation-states accumulating Bitcoin proves true, we could be witnessing one of the most significant developments in Bitcoin's history. A supercycle driven by international demand could see Bitcoin's value reach unprecedented levels, solidifying its place as a global asset.

OTHER CRYPTOS

Amid a plethora of "cryptocurrencies" that have been introduced, none have garnered the magnitude or quality of energy that Bitcoin attracts. Many other cryptos are like penny stock scams, luring energy through enticing sales tactics, but their primary beneficiaries are typically the original creators and owners. For example, DogeCoin was first offered as a joke and not as any real monetary system based on sound protocols or cryptographic achievements. Sadly, many investors who buy into these scams seeking a quick buck often find themselves on the losing end.

There are some tokens associated with other blockchains (such as Ethereum or Solana) that developers are using as platforms for various technologies, smart contracts, and the tokenization of other assets. While these platforms may be useful technologies that add value, they are very different from Bitcoin. While they also have tokens or "coins" associated with them, they do not have Bitcoin's features (which have the potential to be the foundation of new sound money).

If these other crypto tokens are viable and useful technologies themselves, why do they need a suspect monetary unit (coin) as part of the technology? They are essentially unregistered securities. They are generally centralized ledgers that typically work on a "proof of stake" model. This means that those who own the coins have a stake and get to make or change the rules, including adding more coins to the system. Unlike Bitcoin these systems require trust in the creators and stakeholders (a dubious proposition) and certainly did not have an "immaculate conception." Even if they may find use as "currencies" embedded within certain systems or could be useful for their blockchain technology, they do not have the necessary features and benefits to be a robust, trustless, permissionless, and immutable ledger of transactions for a new system of sound money. A gaming token might be useful within a multiplayer online game, but it is not going to serve as a new global base layer of money!

BITCOIN'S DECENTRALIZED NETWORK

The distinctive feature of Bitcoin is the absence of a central authority or promoter. It is a decentralized network following common protocols. While there are self-interested promoters, traders, and fraudsters in any system, the fundamental structure of the Bitcoin network sets it apart. The value and strength of the network increase as more people use it, but the protocols and the limits on Bitcoin creation are fixed and stable features.

This is unlike other systems, where those who control the network get to set and change the rules. Again, this may be fine for a technology platform but not for a new base layer of money. That's why those who truly understand Bitcoin refer to these other coin schemes as "shitcoins" when they are proffered as competitors or alternatives to Bitcoin.

The value of a network hinges on the perception of its usefulness; thus, its value increases as adoption grows. The network's worth—its gravitational pull—is derived from its ability to provide a valuable service to people. Just as email systems wouldn't have flourished if people didn't see the value in sending emails instead of traditional letters, the Bitcoin protocols and network gain value because individuals recognize their utility and choose to store energy with them. However, it's crucial to remember that, much like emails or letters, what matters lies in the message and not in the means of transport. However, some technologies are better ways of relaying the message with greater speed, security, and integrity.

Imagine being in captivity and having to send a letter through your captor, fully aware that your message might not make it through. Since you are a prisoner, your message is vulnerable to confiscation, redaction, or even destruction. The system lacks security, privacy, and integrity. As fiat currencies evolve into fully digital and programmable units, such as central bank digital currencies (we'll discuss these more in chapter 18), our value storage device (money) starts to resemble a prisoner's letter. We lose control over the transmission and storage of the productive value of our efforts and messages. Instead, they become subject to the objectives of the state rather than those of the individual.

In the Bitcoin network, the nodes (discussed in chapter 14) verify transactions before they are added to the blockchain of transactions. There are well over ten thousand active nodes in approximately one hundred countries worldwide. Only with consensus approval (a vote, if you will) of the decentralized nodes can a new block be created and affirmed. Illegitimate transactions or those that do not conform to the protocols are rejected. This is what makes Bitcoin a distributed and decentralized network. No single ledger controls transactions, so past transactions (blocks) cannot be altered. If a number of nodes go down, for example, due to a local power outage, many more are still operating to support the network. Since every node maintains a full copy of the blockchain, even a catastrophic event that wipes out many nodes will allow the recovery and reestablishment of an extensive network verifying the accuracy of the historic blockchain and ready to approve new transactions. If J. P. Morgan's ledger goes down, good luck figuring out and proving what money you had with them!

AN EVOLVING BATTERY OF MONEY

Each person's work can be considered a form of property interest. We all understand that when someone writes a book or composes music, this work is considered their intellectual property. It is something that they claim a property right to. So, it's also important to understand that Bitcoin is more than money or a currency. As a store of value, it is a form of property. As Michael Saylor wrote on X on March 11, 2024, "Bitcoin is Digital Property. It is superior to other investments such as Gold, Equity, or Real Estate because it is digital, available, global, ethical, & useful to millions of companies and billions of people." He has called Bitcoin the "apex property of the human race."

The crucial question is where do you prefer to store your

energy? Consider what features of a monetary battery appeal to you. Do you wish for your energy to be preserved rather than dissipated? Would you like the ability to control and transfer it without relying on someone else's permission? Is minimizing the risk of your energy being blocked from transmission or confiscated important to you? While these concerns may have once seemed remote for most people in developed Western economies, they are becoming increasingly relevant. Ultimately, wouldn't you choose to secure the fruits of your labor in the "apex property of the human race?"

MONETARY CONTROLS

For those who live in authoritarian countries and failing economies, monetary concerns are literally a matter of life and death. Failing currencies fail their citizens. They rob them of the productive efforts of their labor, often in favor of propping up and serving the whims and power of dictators and those in their favor. Yet, what once seemed something distant and remote to those in the Western world is now coming closer.

Freezing and seizing assets, regulating how and what you can do with your money, limiting funds transfers, and requiring government reporting on transactions are now the norm in most countries. Governments argue that these measures counter criminal activity, but when the rights and privacy of law-abiding citizens are compromised, often without evident cause, it's our freedom that becomes the casualty. It's important to remember that the state determines who is labeled a criminal and that, in authoritarian regimes, the exercise of free speech, movement, and the ease of money transfer is swiftly compromised.

Freedom and liberty are things most humans crave, even if

our starting places may be different. One view holds that they are innate human rights that should be infringed upon only lightly. Another view is that these are privileges bestowed or denied by a king or state. They are either inalienable human rights that must only be tread on lightly or are rights granted or withheld by the government. Our perspective on this will guide the place we start in constructing a balance between the needs of the individual and the community we are part of. I side with the former. As the famous American attorney Clarence Darrow noted, "You can only protect your liberties in this world by protecting the other man's freedom. You can only be free if I am free."

Imperfect systems are the result of imperfect humans with different perspectives operating together. It is both a beautiful and, at times, ugly picture. The best we can do is to strive to create systems that honor everyone's rights and liberties. If the underlying system is corrupted by "software bugs" that allow nation-states and authoritarian actors to exploit the energy and stores of energy of the citizenry, it is the populace that pays the price. Living together involves respecting individual autonomy and integrity by making compromises to allow diverse members of society to pursue both individual and collective interests. Until all humanity is perfect in each and everyone else's eyes, there will be no perfect system.

A system driven by greed, avarice, and the thirst for power is bound to succumb to corruption. Even the most well-crafted systems will falter if integrity, respect, and love are not their guiding principles. While creating better systems and protocols doesn't guarantee perfection, it certainly increases the likelihood of better outcomes.

For those unfamiliar with Bitcoin, it's crucial to grasp that it provides more than just a means to store wealth or make payments. For those already part of the Bitcoin network who appreciate its ethos, it's essential to be guided by love rather than anger, hatred, or a lack of appreciation for humanity's diversity. Our opportunity and challenge lie in ensuring that a well-engineered monetary system is driven by the most powerful force—love. Because, Tina, love has everything to do with it!

4

War and Peace—and Money

War is a matter not so much of arms as of money. —THUCYDIDES

THE US DOLLAR DRAWS ENERGY globally because people see it as one of the most useful currencies available. Being the most economically and militarily dominant country of the past century has granted the United States immense influence, not only in cultural values but also in mercantilism. The military might of the United States enables the dollar to wield a significant impact worldwide.

While the average user of the dollar might not immediately connect the dots, the ultimate backbone of the currency is the dominance of the United States military. Whether it's exerting power through direct conflict or ensuring the security of shipping and transportation channels, the United States military's strength is a primary factor in what supports the value of its currency.

Before the United States ascended to the position of dominant global power, such power was held by Britain in the eighteenth and nineteenth centuries, the Dutch and Portuguese empires before that, the Roman and Greek empires, and numerous other powers in antiquity. And each of these significant powers wielded the dominant global currency. Might may not make right, but it can make the money.

A significant contrast between historical empires and our present situation, though, is that, for them, gold served as the basis of money. It is no surprise that the Spanish and Portuguese quested for gold in South America or that conquering armies always plundered the gold of defeated enemies. While government coins stamped with their rulers dominated global trade, they were still coins made of gold or silver—the real money. When centralized ledgers, paper notes, and other work-arounds to transferring actual gold came into greater use, governments found new ways to misrepresent how much money (gold) they had or reduced the amount of precious metals in the coins while trying to pass them off for the same value.

While important achievements may not have otherwise occurred if not for this system, its primary benefits—the power of the money—accrue to whatever government has the power of the sword. Henry Kissinger infamously said, "Who controls the food supply controls the people; who controls the energy can control whole continents; who controls money can control the world."

The energy stored and available to a nation experiences significant network effects when a nation's currency becomes widely used beyond its borders. But when military might is a key source of a currency's power, that influence comes at a great cost. The expense of funding widespread military endeavors has bankrupted many an empire. When the power of a currency depends less on the value created by the nation's citizens and it's integrity as a store of value is compromised because it relies on costly military endeavors that lead to the debasement of its currency, that currency's value as sound money declines.

THE CITIZENS WON'T FUND WAR, SO THE GOVERNMENT WILL

Wars require tremendous resources, often beyond the coffers of a nation-state's treasury or its ability to contemporaneously tax its citizens. When kings or states ran out of money, they ran out of munitions, so the war ended. While history has seen protracted conflicts, the course of intense fighting was usually more limited as funds eventually ran out. With the advent of an extensive credit/debt-based system, government borrowing became a useful vehicle to raise money for war. Hence, the origin of war bonds. If the citizens support the war effort, they will buy the bonds. But if they don't, what's the government to do?

In his book, *The Fiat Standard: Debt Slavery Alternative to Human Civilization*, Saifedean Ammous describes the manipulation and financial treachery surrounding the issuance of Britain's first war bond to raise money for WWI.

In November 1914, the British government issued the first war bond, aiming to raise £350 million from private investors at an interest rate of 4.1% and a maturity of ten years. Surprisingly, the bond issue was undersubscribed, and the British public purchased less than a third of the targeted sum. To avoid publicizing this failure, the Bank of England granted funds to its chief cashier and his deputy to purchase the bonds under their own names. *The Financial Times*, ever the bank's faithful mouthpiece, published an article proclaiming the loan was oversubscribed. John Maynard Keynes worked at the Treasury at the time, and in a secret memo to the bank, he praised them for what he called their "masterly manipulation." Keynes's fondness for surreptitious monetary arrangements would go on to inspire thousands of economic textbooks published worldwide. The Bank of England had set the tone for a century of central bank and government collusion behind the public's back. *The Financial Times* would only issue a correction 103 years later, when this matter was finally uncovered after some sleuthing in the bank's archives by some enterprising staff members and published on the bank's blog.

FUNDING FOREVER WARS

Sadly, as history has shown, governments' ability to manipulate the monetary system and create fake money is often used to further political or military purposes. Unconstrained by the citizenry's voluntary (or coerced) contributions of actual energy through taxes to fund military expenditures, governments often create money to fund wars.

History is replete with wars that the populace would not likely have consciously and willingly paid for. When they are "paid for" through the insidious tax of inflation thanks to currency debasement, then governments are more likely to engage in wars the population would otherwise refuse to fund. If people had to check a box on a tax return and indicate how much additional tax they wanted to pay to fund the war in _____, how much money do you think that would raise? Governments know the answer, so they no longer try to raise money through war bonds. The last war bonds issued by the United States were during World War II. Instead of special-purpose war bonds, funding wars has become part of regular Treasury bond issuance and government operation.

Alex Gladstein of the Human Rights Foundation framed it this way in a March 2, 2022, article in *Bitcoin Magazine* titled "The Invisible Cost of War in the Age of Quantitative Easing":

> One of the hallmark features of democracy is that citizens should, in theory, have a way to prevent their government from waging and prolonging unpopular wars. Through elected representatives, free media, and dialogue around public spending, the argument goes that citizens of democracies should be more directly involved in war making. And if more countries become democracies, there will be less war, as democracies do not historically fight each other.
>
> The problem is that this concept, known as "democratic peace theory," is in danger of failing. As a result of the current dollar framework—in which America's post-9/11 wars in Iraq, Afghanistan, and beyond have effectively been paid for by borrowing—the U.S. may have already lost one of the greatest benefits of democracy: its promise of peace.

He goes on to summarize his thesis as follows:

- Post-9/11 wars have been paid for entirely through borrowing/money printing. These wars have become increasingly distant from daily life and public discourse.

- The US government has engaged in unprecedented intervention in the bond markets, which has helped keep the price of borrowing for war low.

- The negative effects of debt-financed war include a rise in income inequality due to asset inflation as well as cyclical economic crises.

- Given that foreign demand for U.S. debt has peaked, the only way to keep this system going is more debt monetization through the issuance of new bonds and quantitative easing (QE).

- Financing war through borrowing makes conflict more likely, endangers democratic peace theory, and ultimately erodes democracy itself.

JUST WARS

There will be moments in history when individuals recognize the imperative to unite and actively protect their safety and core principles. In the face of genuine existential dangers, the general public is willing to take essential measures. Perhaps there may one day be a war that the American people, in the tradition of World War II, would willingly enter into with their own blood and treasure to defend democracy. Maybe, like Pearl Harbor, Americans would wait to engage until the United States was attacked directly. Any broadly popular war in any nation could be fought under any monetary standard.

However, numerous conflicts are entered into not from a genuine necessity for collective defense but due to leaders, politicians, and corporate cronies striving to assert and broaden their power and influence. Whether it is an eagerness to secure economic benefits through military strength, the desire to exert control over natural resources, or a propensity for war fueled by the influence of the military-industrial complex, much of the benefits accrue to large military, construction, and energy producers and not to the citizen who bears the opaque financial burden of the costs of war or the tangible horrors of the loss of life. And nowhere is there concern or respect for the cultural and moral foundations of others.

Only the fiat standard makes forever wars in the Middle East and Asia, disconnected from the lives of average Americans and Europeans, possible. In short, the true cost of war can be made dangerously invisible in democracies today. But it does not have to be forever. Under a Bitcoin standard, such wars would likely be rejected.

BRING ME A HIGHER LOVE

In our current fiat system, the energy that most people would prefer to see directed to sustain their families, neighbors, and communities is increasingly diverted to acts of aggression. People are inherently good, and while ignorance and manipulation can distort their use of energy, our fundamental desires are much the same. Most of us wish to live peacefully and have adequate food, water, clothing, and shelter to care for ourselves and others, and share and celebrate the magnificent gift of life. It is institutions, politicians, and governments that may have other objectives or twist these human desires to suit their purposes.

Nation-states, as they currently exist, are a recent historical development. While cultural and historical affinities between peoples exist, and nation-states do serve a purpose in the world we live in today, many existing national borders are artificial constructs resulting from wars or colonialism. In a new global age, we have the opportunity to think beyond the confines of a nation-state-centric world. We live in both a global world and also one where true community consists of those whom we are closest to (whether geographically or not). Many people within existing countries may have little in common other than the borders of the nation-state. Fervent nationalism in our existing nation-state system is often used by rulers to perpetuate cycles of power, dominance, and conflict.

Author Arundhati Roy put it this way in her book *War Talk*:

> Nationalism of one kind or another was the cause of most of the genocide of the twentieth century. Flags are bits of colored cloth that governments use first to shrink-wrap people's minds and then as ceremonial shrouds to bury the dead.

If we move beyond currencies dominated and manipulated by nation-states, we can also move beyond the limitations of a primary national identity. This identity, which is generally a matter of birth location and not choice, defines wars we may be conscripted to fight in as well as our freedom of movement. A leader's lust for power can cost ordinary citizens their lives whether they believe in the cause or not.

The free movement of money and capital can also pave the way for the freer movement of people. It has become a normal part of life in the last hundred years or more that you must "show your papers" to cross borders, which is a means of control. There are valid reasons in today's world to have border controls due to the wide disparity in political, economic, and human rights conditions between countries. If we move to a global system of money, the control and pressures exacted by capital controls, hyperinflation, and currency manipulation can help remove one source of the desire of citizens to flee failing states. Few people choose to leave their homelands without good reason. We must address the root causes of these issues, which result in tragic migration and mass refugee situations.

There are no simple answers, but to begin to deconstruct existing structures and build new ones that better serve humanity, we need to think beyond the limitations of our existing global nation-state order. But that does not mean some dystopian new world order of the global elite. What we create should be a product of the dreams and ambitions that support all people. As Pakistani Nobel Prize winner Malala Yousafzai said, "Let us make our future now, and let us make our dreams tomorrow's reality."

Saifedean Ammous, in his seminal work, *The Bitcoin Standard*, wrote:

> Civilization is not about more capital accumulation per se; rather, it is about what capital accumulation allows humans to achieve, the flourishing and freedom to seek higher meaning in life when their base needs are met and most pressing dangers averted.

When we can satisfy our basic needs, we can, as Mr. Ammous notes, delve deeper into the "higher meaning of life" and, as we will discuss later, ascend Abraham Maslow's pyramid toward self-actualization. Everything many of us do, all our labor, all the work we do to grow food, build roads and shelter, develop new technologies, and engineer new and better ways of using the resources of this planet are directed toward satisfying our basic needs so we can seek this higher meaning. Understanding that we all live in an interconnected and interdependent web of life with energy as its basis provides a foundational place upon which to work individually and cooperatively so we can achieve these common needs and goals.

The clarity and strength of the signals we generate and share are a function of the purity of the proof of work and proof of love we demonstrate and offer. The more the signals are diluted, distorted, and unbacked by actual proof of work, the more interference is introduced that dissipates the value of our energy and the value of our love. When there is no real work and no real love, then what is created is not a pretty sight.

If we are tuned in to politicians and media and the frequencies of fear they generate—anger, uncertainty, and doubt—then that is the information we have to work with. We retransmit and amplify these messages so that the vibrational field of anxiety grows stronger. The primitive brain tends toward the negative to assess threats and protect us. Signals that trigger the fight-or-flight mode or a trauma response keep us trapped in a limited vibrational frequency. Operating from a vibration of fear and judgment shapes our experience of life and the world we create. If we tune in to the frequency of understanding, peace, compassion, and love, we will have a very different life experience.

THE FREQUENCY OF PEACE

It takes the elevation of our consciousness (our receiver) to avoid the lower frequencies around us and, instead, pick up on higher wavelengths. Spiritual and religious masters throughout the ages have provided guidance and pathways to help us tune in to these signals. Whether it is meditation, devotion, prayer, contemplation, ritual, or a myriad of other practices, these are methods of tuning out lower frequencies and tuning in to higher and more subtle ones.

To create a more peaceful world, we must create a more peaceful mindset. Peace, like love, starts as an inside job and spreads out. Suppose we imagine and build new systems based on the mindset that they must contribute to the possibility of a more peaceful world, not on how they divide us or can be used to accumulate more power and control by a few. We can focus on something "out there" not being right, but we may miss the opportunity to ensure that what's inside is properly aligned with leading a peaceful life.

Lao Tzu put it this way:

If there is to be peace in the world,
    There must be peace in the nations.
If there is to be peace in the nations,
    There must be peace in the cities.
If there is to be peace in the cities,
    There must be peace between neighbors.
If there is to be peace between neighbors,
    There must be peace in the home.
If there is to be peace in the home,
    There must be peace in the heart.

When we reflect on what money really is—a transmitter of our energy—as well as on what signals we transmit and focus on, we may find that we are tuning in to only one frequency. Are we being manipulated by the messages of someone else's agenda, or are we tuning in to our own inner wisdom and higher-frequency transmissions? What frequency is that? Is it the frequency of peace? Is it the frequency of love? It is only from these frequencies that we can create a freer, fairer, and more peaceful and loving world.

5

The Love in Money

Money is life energy that we exchange and use as a result of the service we provide to the universe. —DEEPAK CHOPRA

NOW THAT WE UNDERSTAND that money is an energetic message transmitted between people, let's look at the nature of this energy. It is a signal, but a signal of what?

WORK IS LOVE

I suggest we consider that everything we do, everything the planet provides, and everything in the universe is simply love—even though it might not always look like it. Human ignorance can frequently distort the signal of love. A survival instinct, a love of life, is inherent within us.

What if we look at energy as another word for love? When we expend energy, it is really an expression of love. When we are using our energy to raise a child, we are doing it as an expression of love. When we work a job to earn money (whether we like the job or not), we do so because we want to live and wish to sustain ourselves, our family, and others we love. Kahlil Gibran summed it up this way in *The Prophet*: "Work is love made visible."

When someone creates a new way of organizing material energy into a product, they do so because they believe that it will be useful to others and that it will provide value to them. When someone paints or composes music, they do so as a creative expression of the energy—love—within themselves. If that frequency resonates with someone else, the perception of beauty is experienced. Listening to your favorite music, looking at an exquisite sculpture or painting, talking on the phone to your child, cooking a meal, sharing intimacy with a lover, or taking a walk in the park can all be an experience of love.

Humans can shift energy patterns to create value for themselves and others. We can pull rocks out of the ground, heat and combine them into steel, and build structures to live in that support life. We can plant seeds in the ground and organize their care, harvesting and delivering the fruits of these efforts to others to nourish and sustain life. We arrange musical notes in patterns that resonate and transmit something more than sound.

If we are mentally and emotionally mature, humans act in ways we believe will advance our desire to lead happy, healthy, and joyful lives. We are all alike in this, even though we may have different talents, preferences, and visions for how we want to live. As the Dalai Lama has said at different times:

- Simply as human beings we are the same. And the eight billion people alive today will only survive by acknowledging that we belong to one human family. This is how we create a truly peaceful world—by keeping in mind what we all have in common and being helpful to each other.

- In our hearts, we all want to live in peace, to be happy and to avoid suffering. This is the basis of our common humanity.

- All human beings, regardless of their status, have the same basic need for love, affection, and respect.

- Rich or poor, educated or uneducated, each human being is essentially the same, and each possesses the same potential for happiness or suffering.

- The more we care for the happiness of others, the greater our own sense of well-being becomes. This is the basis of inner peace and happiness, not wealth or status.

DISTORTED MONEY, DISTORTED LOVE

While love doesn't require effort and is present in all of us, in practice, we often lose sight of this. The love that flows from us as we express our creativity, care for and interact with others, and find our path in life can be blocked by false narratives and transactional, credit/debt approaches to life. Like the government printing fiat money that distorts the energy of work, the veil of our conditioning and trauma distorts our vision of what love really is. Ignorance casts a shadow that can inhibit clearly seeing the nature of reality and authentic relationships.

While we don't have to work for love, we often do have to work to cast off our illusions. Sharing love also takes the strength to be vulnerable. We often fear the apparent hurt that can come with real vulnerability. Like people who hoard money or possessions out of fear, thinking it will protect them from harm, donning emotional armor to prevent us from being hurt also prevents us from truly experiencing and sharing love. We clog the energy stream—the free and easy flow of love—when we erect barriers to it.

As the old expression goes, to be able to receive, you must be able to give. But if you give what is not actually yours, it is a false expression, and everyone gets robbed. Pretending one can create and distribute money or wealth with no basis in real work that creates real products from human energy is a fallacy that corrupts and distorts the system.

In the famous allegory by Plato, a group of men are kept in a cave since childhood as prisoners. Chained, they can only stare at shadows on the wall in front of them projected from behind them. All they know are shadows, so they seem real. Then, when one man is freed and leaves the cave, he experiences true light and reality. He then understands the illusions he has been deluded by. When he returns to the cave to share this insight with others, they do not believe him and prefer to turn back and stare at their comfortable shadows.

And like the allegory, when we have grown up in a fiat system with all its economic models and theories, it is hard to discern the shadow nature of what is happening and to take the scary journey of escaping to the light of truth. Arriving at fully comprehending the fiat standard is a journey that is much like freeing ourselves of the shackles that keep us chained and staring at shadows. It is possible, though, to gain such knowledge and understanding, stepping out of the cave into unfamiliar territory and the light of truth. And it is from this place that we can share and embrace new systems and new possibilities for a freer, fairer, and more peaceful world.

6

It's High Time to Get Low

Time is the moving image of eternity. — **PLATO**

TIME PREFERENCE IS A CONCEPT that originated in economics to address whether people value present ends or future ends. It is the inclination and incentives for people to focus their efforts on the short-term satisfaction of wants or to defer gratification and be oriented to the longer term. Focusing on short-term gratification is known as having a high time preference. In other words, "When do we want it? We want it now!" There is less concern with the longer term and the consequences of our actions in the future than with obtaining what we want currently. There's a saying: "No one ever washed a rental car." When we aren't invested in something for the long term, we tend to have little regard for its care or maintenance.

These economic terms (high and low time preference) can seem confusing. Just think of it this way. When people have a long-term perspective, they are willing to forgo something now (the time factor) for a better future. This is a low time preference. If the bias is toward the short term, they place a high value on getting it now, so they have a high time preference. High time preference = short-term thinking. Low time preference = long-term thinking.

CONSUMPTION AND DEBT OR SOMETHING DEEPER

Our credit/debt-based monetary system exacerbates the tendency toward short-term thinking and a consumption orientation. Why wait to get something until you can actually pay for it when you can buy it on credit and have it today? Debt-fueled systems encourage immediate gratification.

Corporate earnings and profits are also driven by short-term thinking. The market focuses on quarterly results, not necessarily on the long-term health of the corporation's balance sheet or its product offerings. An "earnings beat" is the holy grail. The system encourages companies to take on debt to finance dividends, share buybacks, or often ill-conceived acquisitions.

Our economists, market theorists, and governments have driven us to be primarily a consumer economy. The dominant economic theory of the last hundred years, Keynesian economics, has measured the state and health of the economy based on total aggregate spending. The more we can spend, the thinking goes, the better off we will be. With approximately 70 percent of the US economy being driven by consumer spending, it's no wonder all the market forces (as well as all the insidious marketing) encourage people to spend now rather than saving for later. When much of the cost of a product is driven by marketing expenses, shouldn't that be telling us something? But buy we must the system says, so if the consumer won't or can't spend, the government will step in.

In such a system, saving is largely discouraged. During the "Great Financial Crisis," driven in large part by leverage and bad loans, the solution was to cut interest rates to get money and spending moving. As evidenced by hedge fund founder Ray Dalio's "cash is trash" axiom, after a decade of 0 percent interest rates, regular people could no longer save their money "safely" without seeing their purchasing power eroded by inflation that was above the rate of interest earned.

Even our education system, which is supposed to demonstrate low time preference behavior—i.e., study and learn now so that you can have a better long-term future—has become a victim of our debt system. Student loan debt saddles our children with an enormous debt burden so that they are forced to focus on jobs that will enable them to pay back their debt rather than on those that nourish their talents. Either that or the government will sweep it all away and forgive the debt that requires more fake government money be printed to pay for it. The educational-industrial complex is focused on creating consumers for their products through debt financing.

Hannah Arendt in *The Human Condition* posits three primary stages of human activity: humans as laborers (*animal laborans*) existing primarily to satisfy basic human needs of food, shelter and reproduction, humans as tool makers (*homo faber*) who fabricate tools and technologies to improve their capacity to satisfy basic needs, and humans taking action unrelated to the end of consumption.

It is this later stage that creates a lasting world beyond the life of an individual and where humanity transcends basic animal needs. It is action in this capacity that creates art, music, and political ideals and strives for immortality. She says, "Action, the only activity that goes on directly between men without the intermediary of things or matter, corresponds to the human condition of plurality." It is in living and acting together for something more than just food or shelter that the true potential of humanity is revealed.

When our primary, if not exclusive, focus is on the marketplace and the world of production and consumption, we limit ourselves from taking action to explore and transcend life beyond our basic needs, which is characteristic of the actions of humans in the stage of laborers and fabricators. As Arendt states:

> One of the obvious danger signs that we may be on our way to bring into existence the ideal of the *animal laborans* is the extent to which our whole economy has become a waste economy, in which things must be almost as quickly devoured and discarded as they have appeared in the world, if the process itself is not to come to a sudden catastrophic end. But if the ideal were already in existence and we were truly nothing but members of a consumers' society, we would no longer live in a world at all but simply be driven by a process in whose ever-recurring cycles things appear and disappear, manifest themselves and vanish, never to last long enough to surround the life process in their midst.

Stepping back from humans as primarily actors in the marketplace to the perspective that consumption is only one facet of existence is a key theme of this book. Our economic structures and monetary systems are crucial to the effectiveness of satisfying our basic needs. We must attend to and continue to progress in our *vita activa*—the active and practical life of labor and technological development to fulfill our basic needs as well as our social and political organization to live together in plurality. Our current monetary and economic systems detract from humanity's ability to better satisfy these needs because of value extractive rather than additive actions and the lack of integrity in our fiat monetary system.

If, instead of perpetual debt burdens that necessitate an inflationary monetary system, we were to embrace a new monetary technology and a new relationship with consumption, we could pave the way for moving beyond a view of life limited to making and consuming material goods. There is still much to do to satisfy the basic needs of all of humanity. But once secured, it is humans as actors in plurality exploring and creating lasting social structures, performing great and heroic deeds, and also engaging in Aristotle's *vita contemplativa* where humanity can realize its potential. For me, this is not the philosopher or hermit's life of withdrawal from the world into thought. Rather, it is the balance between resting in the stillness of being and then, from that place, taking action to rise up to meet the needs of the hour. When we pursue wisdom in thought and action, we can find joy that transcends anything found in material goods or the marketplace.

LASTING QUALITY IS GONE

Cheap words, like cheap goods, don't have much meaning and don't last. Planned obsolescence—the idea that goods are intentionally designed to become outdated or useless in a brief time period—is classic high time preference thinking. It is the waste economy Arendt referred to. When we are engaging in the life of producing and consuming, we can at least do it with quality, integrity, and a higher time preference perspective.

As any consumer can attest, the quality of finished goods has steadily declined. As we substitute cheap disposable items for well-made, long-lasting products, the system demonstrates its preference for "give it to me now" products (regardless of how crappy they are) rather than a focus on high-quality, long-lasting goods that may cost more in the short term but save money in the long term.

The same is true in the arts. How many formulaic movie sequels do we need, and what do they really contribute other than generating box office receipts? Much of our entertainment, music, and television culture is filled with distractions and spectacles that divert us from the reality of serious social, political, and economic issues.

As for architecture, well, look at the buildings of antiquity still standing compared to the shopping malls or office buildings we build now that are torn down in a matter of a few decades. Many of civilization's great monuments and buildings have remained standing for hundreds and even thousands of years. Yet, today, it seems that we are unable to build things that last more than a few decades, if that.

Our agricultural and food industries are mainly focused on maximizing short-term production at the expense of soil sustainability and food and nutrient quality. Now we have factory farming—the term itself says it all. Whether you are a carnivore, a vegetarian, or a vegan, what passes for food in most supermarkets is not designed to maintain the body's long-term health. As Zach Bush, MD, said about the technological takeover of our food system and biome, "We have chosen technology over biology."

Matthew Lysiak and Saifedean Ammous in *Fiat Food: Why Inflation Destroyed Our Health and How Bitcoin Fixes It* explore the depths of the deception and the false narrative that has been created around what constitutes a healthy diet. "Our food system in America has been hijacked by corporate enterprises looking to profit." They arrive at a surprising source for why the narrative about what healthy food is has changed, "When the money printer was pointed in the direction of the food supply, there were consequences to food quality that were driven by a desire to hide inflation."

Factory-made and processed food can be produced more abundantly and cheaply than wholesome, traditional real food. The food pyramid is really a marketing effort to drive people away from higher-quality but more expensive food and toward cheap, nutritionally dubious food. The now apparent ramifications of this are the rising levels of obesity, chronic disease, and poor health we see, particularly in the United States. This is a clear example of short-term thinking and a high time preference orientation of a fiat system costing us all far more than just economically. All this again reveals the depth of the impact of a corrupted inflationary monetary system.

It all recalls Juvenal's critique of the Roman populace only caring about "bread and circuses" because the Roman elite manipulated the populace with cheap food and entertainment to retain power and control and to pacify and distract them from calling for meaningful change.

Allen Farrington and Sacha Meyers's book *Bitcoin Is Venice* provides a thorough discussion of how the high time preference mindset of our fiat monetary, debt-based system has affected farming and soil depletion. Farmers are driven to take out large loans to buy more land, equipment, fertilizer, and high-priced corporate-manufactured seed, forcing them to increase yields beyond what is sustainable to generate the income to pay back the loans. Soil is literally capital, they explain, and we are destroying it rapidly by degenerate fiat finance and money.

And then there is our medical system, where we focus not on health and well-being (low time preference) but on drugs, surgery, and disease management for critical and chronic health issues. In conjunction with our industrial-agriculture system, we are sowing the seeds of ever-increasing poor health. All of which necessitates ever-increasing government spending of printed money to pay increasingly obscene medical costs. Perversely, increasing medical expenses (irrespective of declining health metrics) result in higher aggregate spending, so it is a net positive for the size of the economy in this bizarre way of looking at what constitutes a healthy system.

A US PRESIDENT'S PRESCIENT WARNING

In President Dwight D. Eisenhower's farewell address before leaving office in 1961, he warned of the dangers of the military-industrial complex. This is rather surprising coming from a US army general and the supreme commander of Allied forces in Europe in World War II. He said as follows:

[An] immense military establishment and a large arms industry is new in the American experience. The total influence—economic, political, even spiritual—is felt in every city, every State house, every office of the Federal government. We recognize the imperative need for this development. Yet, we must not fail to comprehend its grave implications. Our toil, resources, and livelihood are all involved. So is the very structure of our society.

But the president spoke about more than the impact of the military-industrial complex. He spoke very deeply and directly about the risks of a high time preference mentality for all spheres of human activity:

As we peer into society's future, we—you and I, and our government—must avoid the impulse to live only for today, plundering for our own ease and convenience the precious resources of tomorrow. We cannot mortgage the material assets of our grandchildren without risking the loss also of their political and spiritual heritage. We want democracy to survive for all generations to come, not to become the insolvent phantom of tomorrow.

Let this sink in. Over sixty years ago, a military commander from the height of the perspective of the presidency of the most powerful country on the planet foresaw and warned of the perils of mortgaging the future and causing the loss of our political and spiritual ideals. Today, it seems like his warning has become a prophecy.

THE ROOTS OF THE HIGH DEBT SYSTEM

So, let's begin our look at the recipe for turning a society into an "insolvent phantom of tomorrow." At its root, our system of fiat currency is a credit/debt system. There is nothing but "full faith and credit" backing our money. This means that every dollar is somebody else's liability. A government-issued currency is a liability of a government, which has a monopoly because of the currency's sole status as "legal tender for all debts, public and private." When you deposit money in the bank, your account gets credited, and it becomes the bank's liability. It is liable to give your money back when you ask for it (well, sort of). When you take a loan out, you get a debt, and the bank gets an asset. There is nothing in a fiat monetary system that isn't a debt or a credit. This is why many turn to hard or "real" assets like real estate, precious metals, collectibles, and scarce tangible goods instead of fiat currency as a better store of value.

When we add on the effect of "fractional reserve banking," the nature of the debt that our system is replete with becomes even more apparent. Many naturally assume that banks are essentially warehouses, safely storing our money, but nothing could be further from the truth. Banks are only required to keep a small fraction, generally 10 percent or less, of depositors' money on hand. The Federal Reserve Bank of St. Louis explained this in *How Banks Create Money* (2020). "Banks create money by making loans; when they make a loan, they credit the borrower's account, which increases the total amount of deposits in the economy." Or, as the Bank of England in *Money Creation in the Modern Economy* (2014) explains, "When banks make loans, they do not lend out existing deposits. Instead, they create new deposits in the process, thus expanding the money supply."

A more critical take on this is from economist Murray Rothbard in *The Case Against the Fed*, who put it this way, "The process of fractional reserve banking is rooted in the false promise that the bank has on hand all the money it owes its depositors, when in fact only a fraction is there." And in an amusing and prescient rebuke to those who claim Bitcoin is a scam, Rothbard, in *The Mystery of Banking*, said: "Fractional reserve banking, therefore, is a shell game, a Ponzi scheme, a fraud in which the depositors are led to believe that they can always get their money back on demand."

What's more astounding is that if a bank actually wanted to fully back its deposits with reserves, the Fed isn't going to cooperate. A Forbes article by James Broughel in April 2023 noted, "Custodia Bank is an example of a bank that accepts deposits and is willing to back up those demand deposits more than one-for-one with reserves. This means that if a run on the bank were ever to occur, Custodia would be able to satisfy all the customer requests. You'd think this would please the Fed, but when the bank applied to become a member of the Federal Reserve System, its application was rejected."

Loans based on reserves are not a bad thing, but we must realize that with fractional reserve banking, the increase in the money supply created by these loans (without real money in reserve) injects massive amounts of leverage and, therefore, risk into the system. It is one thing if you are an investor tactically accepting the risks posed by using leverage, but it is quite another if you just want to keep your money safe in the bank. When people lose confidence in banks, they want to withdraw their money, and when everyone wants to do this at the same time, there is a "run on the bank," but the money isn't there.

After the Great Depression in the United States, which

rippled worldwide, the US government attempted to restore faith in the system by creating deposit insurance. It was a sales job to convince people that if a bank had a problem, the government would pay you back. It has worked to maintain confidence in the system and has been helpful when small banks have failed due to bad loans or regional economic conditions. But what happens when the problems and bank runs get bigger?

Does the government have the money to pay us all back in the event of a major problem? Well, yes and no. They don't have the money in a vault. In fact, in the United States, the Federal Deposit Insurance Corporation only has reserves of a small percentage of the deposits in the system. So, when the shit hits the fan, the government creates new money and bails out the banks. We've seen this time and time again. And, as the crises get worse and worse, the costs of these bailouts skyrocket. Governments can do this because there is no limitation on their ability to create new units of currency.

At one time, currencies were backed by gold or silver and convertible into it. Yet when money became separated from some natural, limited, physical substance, it was no longer "hard money" and instead became a credit/debt system. While we can no longer convert paper into gold, the fact that governments continue to hold gold reserves suggests that even they know their paper isn't real money.

Money is essentially just a giant ledger allowing us to keep track of our energy. When the fiat currency system made the government the holder of the ledger and gave it the ability to create more currency, we adopted a monetary system that had benefits over a gold-based system but at an increasingly high cost.

Think about it for a minute. One of the premier marks of distinction in our financial system is having a high credit score.

This means the more money the system will loan you, the more "worthy" you are. The greater the system sees you as having the potential to take on lots of debt, then the more access to money you can have.

Now, if you are in tough circumstances and need access to a loan, it is a lot harder to get. The worst aspects of the credit system are seen in the exorbitant interest rates on credit cards and other types of debt, such as payday and car title loans. Those hooked into this system often become debt slaves. The only people who don't seem to worry about paying back big loans are the banks that get bailed out and the governments that accumulate more debt than can ever be paid off in comparable value.

The United States' national debt has exploded in the last few years to over $36 trillion. That's over $100,000 per citizen and over $266,000 per taxpayer. The Congressional Budget Office, even under the rosiest of scenarios, sees no end in sight to the escalation of the national debt. The single largest expense category in the United States' discretionary budget (not required payments like Social Security) is now interest on the national debt. Yes, interest costs are now more than the United States' gigantic defense budget (which is larger than the next nine countries combined). And this is just federal government debt. If we add in the private debt people owe, the US debt number triples. This is all without even considering the unfunded liabilities of Social Security, Medicare, Medicaid, and government pensions. And then there is state and local government debt in the United States, global corporate debt, and the debt of nation-states worldwide, which are often even far worse than in the United States. That weight on Atlas's shoulders is now our debt.

Can you imagine a household budget where you spend more on credit card interest than on rent, food, or transportation?

Imagine a family sitting down for a financial meeting and seeing that their debt exceeds their entire annual income. Their interest costs keep increasing and taking a larger and larger slice of their income. Then, they decide on the brilliant plan of applying for another credit card!

It reminds me of a line from Dr. Seuss's book, *The Cat in the Hat*: "And this mess is so big / And so deep and so tall, / We cannot pick it up. / There is no way at all!"

OK, Tina's singing her song again, "What's Love Got to Do with It."

TIME PREFERENCE IMPACTS RELATIONSHIPS

A system focused on the short term (high time preference) instead of the long term (low time preference) has many consequences. If someone concentrates their energy on the short term, they might think that a one-night stand is a great use of their energy. Picking someone up at a bar and having sex in the car is a high time preference behavior. High time preference biases people to satisfy their needs and desires in the moment.

Alternatively, with a long-term time preference, we might think that a committed relationship is more desirable. Courting someone over months or years, getting married, and having children is a low time preference behavior. I'm not moralizing here on whether one is right or wrong—just pointing out that the focus of our time preference will impact our behavior.

The proof of work and energy involved in these two approaches are vastly different. In the first case, one only has to think long enough to pay the bar tab and get someplace to have sex. In the latter case, the thought process is very different. Can and how will we live and work together for many years as we contribute to each other's happiness? The behavior, decisions, and consequences involved will be very different.

Like our monetary system, many aspects of our relationships are broken. When relationships are transactional instead of relational, we can suffer from being manipulated and exploited. Our relationships never reach the deeper level intimacy and mutuality possible. (I talk more about intimacy in chapter 16.)

When someone views their relationships with a high time preference, the perspective is, What can I get out of this person now? They think little of the impact of their actions on others in the short or long run because they are focused on getting what they want in the shortest period possible. Some people are less interested in expending energy to nourish and foster others than they are in extracting value from them. High time preference behaviors clog the flow of energy and love in all relationships.

Alternatively, when we work on ourselves and are patient with others while they do their work (or not), we are demonstrating a low time preference orientation. Healthy relationships take work. We all have baggage, so working through the suitcase of emotional traumas, conditioned behaviors, and defense mechanisms with each other takes real work. If we don't expend the energy and contribute this proof of work, our relationships will be, at best, limited in depth and, at worst, volatile, adding more unhealthy emotions to our suitcases of wounds.

Just as rain falling on mountaintops flows into streams and rivers in greater and greater volumes, the energy of love accumulates and grows. When we add our love to the river, rather than only taking from it, there is more for all of us to drink from.

Short-term thinking and its concomitant high time preference behaviors emphasize extracting value now rather than increasing the overall value in the system. Ultimately, our sense of being guided by love or greed will contribute to whether we are trying primarily to extract or add value.

The traditional wedding vow, "Until death do us part," is a low time preference commitment. Can you imagine the vow being, "Until I change my mind or find someone better"? Things happen, and people change; some grow and evolve, while others don't, so that the vows may no longer serve our highest good. However, the intent of a vow, a promise, or a commitment loses its meaning if we don't have the intention at the time of making it to keep it and that it will be enduring.

CORRUPTED MONEY, CORRUPTED GOVERNMENT

As we have seen, when it comes to love and money, short-term thinking encourages us to think about what we can take from a system rather than about how to contribute to it and increase flow. The short-term politically advantageous temptation to interfere in the pure flow of energy with made-up money pollutes and dilutes the stream of the real energy of human activity.

Money created and used to curry political favor and dispense government largesse in exchange for votes is corruption. One would think that a government "by the people" would mean that the people affirmatively concur on how their value contributions (through taxation) support the common good. When governments expend resources far beyond what the citizenry is willing to support, we no longer have a government of the people. When people think the government can give them everything, we have a fallacious dependency that will rob everyone of their freedom, liberty, and the benefits of true proof of work. Bread and circuses helped destroy the Roman civilization, not create it.

A high time preference encourages people to extract what they can now from society, industry, the planet, and each other rather than build sustainable and lasting structures to support future generations. Public debts incurred beyond anyone's ability to repay them with comparable value will be defaulted on either explicitly or surreptitiously through the devaluation of money by inflation.

Like a pimp who siphons off money in exchange for protection, a government siphons off value from its citizens' labor through insidious inflation. And with both, there is the unspoken threat of violence if one does not adhere to the rules of the system.

"A government is an institution that holds a monopoly on the legitimate use of violence," said Max Weber. A surefire way to end up in jail is to fail to comply with the rules of the government. While imprisoning someone for crimes against other citizens, such as assault, robbery, and murder, is a legitimate use of the state's authority that most people would agree with, imprisonment for crimes against the state is in another category. Where once Daniel Ellsberg was hailed as a hero for releasing the Pentagon Papers, which outlined the US government's systematic lies during the Vietnam War, now others are vilified and imprisoned for exposing the truth about government activities and crimes.

Energy moves according to the laws of nature. Love is the field from which this energy arises and is transmitted at various frequencies. Our current corrupted fiat monetary system is an inefficient distribution system for the sharing of this energy between people. When all energy is controlled by a centralized system that dilutes everything that flows through it, power and energy are lost. When the central authority stands in the middle of value exchanges, it is subject to temptation and is corruptible.

The evidence is clear that corruption is endemic in most governments around the world.

Expending tremendous resources on disposable actions or unwise investments directed by a government and not the market squanders resources. Building cities and apartment complexes only for them to be unoccupied and then torn down shortly after construction can hardly be construed as a wise use of resources. Yet, we see this occur in China, the world's second-largest economy. In the United States, spending public money so that roadside signs display the name of the current state governor only to have to change them a few years later is an abuse of public resources. When governments or politicians use "our" money for their self-aggrandizement or to build "bridges to nowhere" to curry votes, this short-term thinking wastes the value of our energy.

100 PERCENT RESPONSIBLE

When people and their governments adopt a mindset of long-term thinking and low time preference actions, great and lasting things can be accomplished. Unlike when a landlord uses the cheapest materials to make a place look acceptable to rent, a long-term mindset is one of offering quality to tenants, as though the owner themself plans to live there. I'm not suggesting we need to go back centuries to when it took decades to build things, but I am trying to illustrate a point.

Our approach to money contributes to our mindset. Our mindset, feelings of responsibility, and connection to others contribute to the nature of our actions. Our actions contribute to the environment we create. Sadhguru, an Indian mystic and teacher in the yogic tradition, suggests we adopt a mindset of:

MONEY, LOVE, AND BITCOIN

"I am 100 percent responsible." My initial reaction to this was probably much like yours: Wait, I'm not responsible for what someone else is doing or the situation they are in.

Sadhguru's point does not refer to what people typically mean by the term "being responsible." He is not saying that something is our fault. Instead, he is advising us to change how we look at things. If our attitude is, "I'm not responsible," then we will take little interest, care, or action in response to what we experience. When tragedies occur, we may not have caused them, but we do have the opportunity to make choices about how we respond. If we see ourselves as "not responsible," we are powerless. If we take ownership of our 100 percent responsibility for how we act and how we respond, we are creators of our experience.

This does not mean we have to act in a certain way in any or every situation. Floods halfway around the world may not be in our sphere of competence or ability to act. Yet, rather than dismissing them as not having anything to do with us, we can at least respond with compassion and consciousness. Then, if so moved, we could organize or donate aid, which is wonderful. If not, that is fine too. The deep meaning and significance of this teaching and this mindset are as profound as it is challenging to adopt.

When we view ourselves as "100 percent responsible," it is more likely than not that we will lean toward low time preference behaviors and actions rather than high time preference ones. In various situations, we may more frequently ask ourselves, What am I adding of value? rather than, What can I get out of this? What if we adopt the mindset and operate according to the framework that we are the creators of our experience, responsible for our actions and their consequences, and that love is the guiding force?

7

I Am Forever Indebted to You

The inflated imitations of gold and silver, which after the rapture are thrown into the fire, all is exhausted and dissipated by the debt. All scrips and bonds are wiped out. At the fourth pillar dedicated to Saturn, split by earthquake and flood: vexing everyone, an urn of gold is found and then restored.

— NOSTRADAMUS

THROUGHOUT MOST OF HUMAN HISTORY, "money" consisted of physical objects: seashells, stones, commodities, and most recently, silver and gold. Paper currencies became a layer built on top of value that was stored in gold because gold was neither easily transported nor transacted with, although it was generally seen as a store of value within and across nations. Its production (and therefore the monetary inflation rate—i.e., the increase in its supply) was limited to how much people could find and mine, historically, that has been about 1.5–2 percent a year. Paper money represented a better transfer technology, but it fundamentally derived value from its being convertible into gold. As J. P. Morgan said in his 1912 testimony to the US Congress, "Gold is money. Everything else is credit."

COMMODITY MONEY IS REPLACED

A little background on how the United States moved from the "gold standard," where the dollar was backed by gold reserves, to a fully fiat currency system is essential to understand. In 1933, US president Franklin D. Roosevelt issued Executive Order 6102, which required all US citizens to hand in their gold and gold certificates to the Federal Reserve to be redeemed for pieces of paper. At the time, gold traded for $20.67 per troy ounce. The following year, the price of gold was set at $35.00 per troy ounce. This was a devaluation of 40 percent of the dollar's gold value. That's right, the government made citizens turn in their gold and then gave them back dollar bills worth 40 percent less in gold. It wasn't so much about the government seizing assets (no one came door-to-door to collect your gold), but because the United States was on the gold standard, this step was taken to enforce a devaluation of the dollar. That was necessary because of massive government spending in the face of the Great Depression. My grandfather, a Ukrainian immigrant tailor, was quite upset that he had to turn over his real money—gold—under the threat of fines and imprisonment.

While citizens were banned from owning gold until 1975, US dollars were still convertible into gold by countries for international trade. However, nations around the world became concerned about the US dollar's stability because of Fed money printing far in excess of its gold reserves. In a bold move, French president Charles de Gaulle sent naval ships to the United States in 1965 to collect gold bullion in exchange for these overvalued dollars. The end of the US-dominated paper-for-gold system was near.

In 1971, President Richard Nixon (formerly vice president under Eisenhower, who issued the prescient warning quoted in the previous chapter) "temporarily" suspended the convertibility of US dollars into gold by other nations, and the long history of commodity money was replaced with a new promise. It was no longer a promise that US dollars could be converted into real money. Now, it was simply a promise that the currency was backed by the "full faith and credit" of the United States. This means that our money is based on the belief ("faith") that the government will preserve the value of our savings so we can use it in the future. Read that last line again and think about it. This is really what we have to have faith in—that the government won't devalue our life's work or savings. Sadly, it is a misplaced faith since, in the last hundred years, the dollar's purchasing power has declined by 99 percent. As we discussed in chapter 2, this is the primary long-term source of consistently persistent inflation despite dramatic improvements in technology and productivity that should be making things cheaper.

In short, we place our money in the hands of the government in exchange for a credit in currency. Today, no countries have currencies based on their convertibility into gold. The other side of credit is debt. Without any underlying thing that backs up the credit, all our money is basically just debt. Charles Dickens amusingly put it this way: "[Credit is a system whereby] a person who can't pay gets another person who can't pay to guarantee that he can pay."

There are many reasons why this system developed, and there are good reasons for using credit/debt systems when using underlying hard money would make transactions cumbersome. Yet, it's essential to understand that what we all accept as money is simply a piece of paper not backed by any commodity or scarce asset and that because the government can create it out of thin air, fiat money contributes to all sorts of issues.

RELATIONSHIPS ON THE FIAT STANDARD

How we operate in our monetary system is one thing, but how we operate in other areas of life is another. Yet, the pervasive effects of the credit and debt system can even impact our view of relationships. Suppose human relationships operated like the monetary system: interactions were simply transactions, and every transaction was backed only by a future promise held on credit to be collected later. What would the social system look like?

What if we collectively operated in a way that if I give you something, I need to receive something back (a credit) in return? That's one thing in economic transactions, but what if this transaction-based mentality seeped into and permeated interpersonal human dynamics outside economic transactions? We'd probably end up with all our interactions being based on the "you scratch my back, and I'll scratch yours" mentality. Everything gets reduced to a debt and credit system.

So, what is your definition and understanding of "love?" Is it a transaction where if someone gives you what you want from them, you will credit them with love? I doubt you'd define it this way, even though we may sometimes have acted this way. Some argue that everything in life and all relationships are simply transactional. I'm sure they probably act that way, but it's not how I want to act. Nor, I ask you to consider, is it the way we will create a better world for all. If we reduce all life affairs to economic events, this transaction mindset is a natural result. Transactions are the modus operandi of the market; however, as discussed in the last chapter, the marketplace is only one aspect of life.

LOVE FREELY GIVEN

Isn't the ideal to give love freely and not just in exchange for something? Most religions and spiritual masters have pretty much taught the same thing: love is not a transaction; it is an inherent and abundant force to be shared generously. Love is the expression of appreciation for and wonder at all life and all beings. If we don't feel or experience that and we aren't willing to share it, we have more work to do. Proof of work in love is our ability to be loving while seeking nothing in return.

Now, I'm not suggesting that we shouldn't have personal boundaries or that we should allow ourselves to be abused by those who haven't demonstrated the value of love. When others act in a transactional manner (generally through ignorance) and seek to extract value from us without contributing or sharing what is truly valuable, we don't have to participate, and we can resist.

Matters of the heart and love are not transactions. Real love is an entirely different matter, and, too often, it is neither offered nor shared. As the saying goes, "You can't buy love." Thinking it's okay to exchange someone's not-based-in-love actions with your based-in-love ones is unwise and unlikely to be successful. Love should be relational, not transactional.

If you pay for sex, you know you are not getting love.

When you have a system based on credit and debt, you should understand that you are not always exchanging the most precious commodities there are—your love and the time you have on earth to deepen and share it—with others doing the same.

The ultimate value each human creates in the world is to express the internal sparks of life and love that are inherent in each of us. Creativity, artistic expression, the desire to improve people's lives, growing food to nourish others, and the creation of businesses to meet human needs are all outward expressions of inner passion.

We all come to the planet in different circumstances, with different gifts and talents, and with different desires for how we express them. Yet, the one value we all seem to seek and wish to share and express is, at its essence, love. The more love we give, the more others share in this abundance and, in a healthy system, share that love back.

Unfortunately, the struggle for survival is so challenging for many that few experience love as a foundation of life. And for others—those who are caught in the trap of consumerism, trauma, and transactional relationships—what is truly important in life is usually forgotten.

By tuning in to higher frequencies like love, we channel our energies to create and add value both now and for the future. For example, when we seek to store the value of our labors because we genuinely care about our children and want to provide them with better opportunities and lives in the future, we are channeling love. However, when we cannot store value reliably and instead accumulate excessive debts, we are robbing them of such a future.

If we contribute little to a romantic relationship and demand that our partner do everything we want, we will deplete the flow of love and burn it out. When one person shares while the other transacts and drains, the relationship (system) operates on two different frequencies, and harmony is lost.

Similarly, well-functioning systems generally have a natural and sustainable state of flow. That flow is disrupted when inputs are limited and outputs are maximized. In the money system, as we accumulate fiat money debt, we restrict the amount of flow available to keep the system in balance. By decoupling money from the constraints of sound money principles, governments create excessive levels of debt and leverage on top of a meager store of value as society seeks to consume as much as it can. We divert resources to pay for present consumption in excess of our inputs and steal from future flow.

CONFUSING VALUE AND PAYMENT

The technology of money is a necessary tool when labor becomes more specialized and the geographic distribution of trade becomes larger. A self-sufficient farmer or small tribal group will have little need for money. On the other hand, as people engage in more specialized labor they need the technology of money as a trade mechanism to meet all their needs. So, humans developed various forms of money to trade for other goods and services. What is not used for consumption can be saved to accumulate wealth.

Many highly valuable activities, however, may have little need for a technology of money. Raising children is one of the highest-value activities of society, yet within a family unit, there is little need to use a monetary system to trade value. One parent may engage in an activity that earns money for goods and ser-vices not available within the productive capacity or talent of the family, while another parent may raise children, care for the home, prepare meals, and create a nurturing community. These activities are extraordinarily valuable and necessary for the family, but money is not needed to "trade" this value within the family.

When we shift our thinking from a focus primarily on obtaining more units of money and instead to how we can add value, we see the technology of money for what it is. It is a tool that is useful in certain circumstances and irrelevant in others. When money is irrelevant and unnecessary, it does not mean an activity is not valuable. It just means that paying for it in a monetary unit has no utility.

When society views all activity through the lens of only valuing the accumulation of money and the more we have, the more "valuable" our activity, we end up with a distorted view of value and wealth. In "traditional" family structures, a man may pursue activities that earn money while a woman may stay home and raise children, care for the home, and create and participate in nurturing and healing community development. While money is a useful tool for trading value for labor outside the affairs of the family, for work within the family and close community, the fact that money is unnecessary means nothing about the actual value of those activities.

When a culture's focus is primarily on money and what generates more money, it has gone far astray from understanding and appreciating what is truly valuable. Conflating situations where money has utility with ones where it does not results in confusing payment for services with the value of services. The fact that a parent is not paid to change diapers or read to a child does not mean the activity does not have value. It's just that money is unnecessary unless such activity is outsourced to someone outside the loving bonds of the family. You pay a babysitter to watch a child, but you do not pay a parent.

It is worth considering if this confusion has led to the devaluing of certain unpaid family roles. In a society where money is a god, is it any wonder that family members who play critically valuable roles but are not directly paid for them may feel "less than" and diminished compared to those who "earn" money? Someone who caretakes a parent or spouse is no less valuable than someone who is a provider of goods and services outside the family. Perhaps this is a source of the devalued feeling many mothers and caretakers may have because they don't "earn" money.

Society's overfocus on accumulating money has widespread and pernicious causes and effects. The inflationary debt-based systems we have created requires many families to have dual incomes to survive (and, of course, so they can both be taxed). And when money is the primary measure of value, those who choose to trade off making money for the critically valuable activities of raising children and contributing to a loving community are viewed as less worthy than a high-wage earner.

The more all family members are forced into being wage earners, the more the nurturing, loving, and educating roles of child-rearing and homemaking are outsourced to other wage earners. Education (if not indoctrination) becomes a role of the state and not of the family and community. Childcare becomes the role of the least-paid among us. The loving bonds and standards of behavior within the family are replaced with rules, protocols, and requirements imposed and enforced by "protective service" agencies of the state.

While we have made great strides in many areas, we can also see decay and decline in the healthy functioning of many aspects of our society and family life. And this has nothing to do with whether a family is "traditional" or not. One size does not fit all. What matters is the health of the family unit in raising and nurturing children and contributing to supportive and healthy communities. How we find a new model for a supportive community structure in this very complex modern age is a challenge we need to address. An important component in creating a new model is to consider how pervasive the impacts of our monetary system are and the confusion between money and true value. There are powerful political and economic forces that discourage such inquiry and dismiss concern about such impacts.

When systems are in place that promote wage slavery to benefit existing power structures so that a majority of people become cogs in the machine of promoting greater "productivity," we lose both individual sovereignty and dignity as well as supportive communities. We need to examine the multilayered nature and cause of such problems and consider the impact our distorted government-controlled monetary system has on the society we are creating. In so doing, answers will lie, in part, in distinguishing between the role of money, the meaning of true value-additive activity apart from money, and the recognition of the responsibility we have as families and communities to ground our structures in principles based on love, integrity, and respect, not control, division, and denigration.

YOU CAN'T FAKE PROOF OF WORK

Since Bitcoin is not based on credit and debt, its system must be fueled by true inputs of value. Bitcoin is "mined" with the expenditure of real costs for the electricity required to solve computational problems and earn the right to add the next block to the blockchain. Miners who have lower electricity costs can devote more resources to the computational energy required to obtain the Bitcoin block reward. This reward is composed of two parts: 1) the block reward in new Bitcoin and 2) the fees associated with the transactions that comprise the block being added to the blockchain.

To obtain scarce Bitcoin, one must input actual energy, whether in the form of the electricity paid for by miners or by purchasing Bitcoin using the stored value (money) of one's labors (of love). Bitcoin requires proof of work, which means real work—real expenditure of energy—is required to participate. New Bitcoin is created according to a strict formula by those who devote substantial resources in the form of electricity to solve complex computations. Unlike fiat currency, which allows a central bank to add digits to financial institutions' accounts or to print more money, creating Bitcoin requires real energy and costs money. It doesn't come for free.

Bitcoin's proof of work system is in contrast to many other cryptocurrencies that operate based on a "proof of stake." Most of these thousands of other cryptocurrencies have been created by some promoter who "made" coins themselves by pushing some buttons. And it just so happened that they gave themselves a whole bunch of them before trying to sell them to others. In addition, the players with the most coins get to make the rules. Once they prove they have a stake—by having a lot of coins— they get to run the show. Does that sound familiar? Isn't that a lot like our current monetary system? Those with the most money get to control things and create the rules.

In a debt-based system, acquiring assets often involves taking on debt. In such a system, when money is created through credit, those near the money printer (the Federal Reserve) are the first recipients of the newly generated money. This occurs when central banks aim to "inject liquidity" into the system. They do this by crediting major commercial banks with additional reserves. The banks then use these reserves to buy assets or make new loans based on this newly credited money. Since they have more reserves, they can loan out more money or buy new assets based on these reserves.

Another circumstance when new money is created is to rescue failing financial institutions. When the fancy term "recapitalized" is used to describe how the government rescues a struggling financial institution, this essentially means that it creates new money to provide to the bank. No one else would put their money into a failing institution, so the government does it to "protect" the system. Simply put, when a failing institution is recapitalized, the government or central bank injects newly created money into it to prevent it from collapsing. The core process does not involve any tangible economic activity; aside from possibly some meetings and press conferences, no actual work occurred to contribute to the overall system.

On a Bitcoin standard, money can't be made up out of thin air like it can be in a fiat system. Actual effort must be expended to acquire it—either through expending energy to mine Bitcoin or by converting your value (energetic output) stored in fiat currency or other assets into Bitcoin. Even though leverage and various complex financial instruments (e.g., options) can be used to acquire an interest in Bitcoin, sooner or later, those liabilities must be converted into real equity, or the interest is lost. No one gets to create Bitcoin without effort. Credit and debt can coexist on top of a system built on a Bitcoin standard, but understand that the foundation is real value and real energy, unlike false money built on debt and controlled by existing extractive power structures. Bitcoin offers the potential to free ourselves from the parasitic financial leeches draining the lifeblood from the economic body of humanity.

8

Energy Use, Sustainability, and Economic Development

The history of civilization is the history of the engineering of energy.

—LYMAN ABBOTT

I MUST ADDRESS THE FALLACIOUS ARGUMENT that Bitcoin should be rejected because the electricity associated with Bitcoin mining will destroy the planet and our environment. Uninformed and biased early studies created exaggerated concern about the impact of Bitcoin mining's energy usage. Yes, Bitcoin requires electricity to run the computers that mine the tokens. Successful miners are those who use the lowest-cost energy available, which is often stranded (unused or wasted) energy. The fact that energy is used to create something validates the integrity of the creation. Humanity has grown and developed because we use more energy, not less.

Electricity usage must be viewed in the context of the value added to society. Electric lights use considerable energy, but few are suggesting we discard lighting. I don't recall seeing any headlines about how air-conditioning or clothes dryers should be abolished because they use too much electricity. The office buildings and computer systems of the thousands of banks and financial institutions that are all part of our fiat currency system consume tremendous amounts of electricity. And as discussed, that system comes at a great cost beyond electricity usage. Energy usage must be considered in the context of costs and benefits.

SENSATIONAL HEADLINES

Critics of Bitcoin also often point to Bitcoin's energy usage as contributing to the potentially catastrophic levels of energy use that may be contributing to climate change. Mainstream media has for years been full of statements such as:

- "Bitcoin Uses More Electricity than Many Countries" (*New York Times*, September 3, 2021)

- Bitcoin's growing energy problem: "It's a Dirty Currency" (*Financial Times*, May 20, 2021)

- "Bitcoin Mining on Track to Consume All of the World's Energy by 2020" (*Newsweek*, December 11, 2017)

- "Bitcoin Will Burn the Planet Down"
  (*Wired*, November 5, 2018)

As Lyn Alden (an investment strategist who also has a background in electrical engineering) notes in "Bitcoin's Energy Usage Isn't a Problem. Here's Why," a white paper first written in 2021 and updated in January 2023:

> It's easier to sensationalize things for pageviews or political gain. For example, it's commonly said that the Bitcoin network uses more energy than some countries. That's true, but then so does Google, YouTube, Facebook, Amazon, the cruise industry, Christmas lights, household drying machines, private jets, the zinc industry, and basically any other sizable platform or industry. From that list, Bitcoin's energy usage is the closest to that of the cruise industry's energy usage, but bitcoins are used by more people, and the network scales far better. If people were 10% more efficient at shutting off their electronic devices when not using them, then that alone would save more energy than the global Bitcoin network uses.
>
> Bitcoin's energy usage is a rounding error as far as global energy usage is concerned. And I mean that literally; when scientists estimate that the world uses a certain amount of energy in a given year, they can easily be off by a couple percentage points in either direction, let alone a couple tenths of a percent. Bitcoin uses less than one tenth of one percent.

BITCOIN'S ENERGY USAGE AS A SOLUTION

An article by Nic Carter, "How Much Energy Does Bitcoin Actually Consume?," in the *Harvard Business Review* in May 2021 framed the issue this way:

> How much energy *should* a monetary system consume?
>
> How you answer that likely depends on how you feel about Bitcoin. If you believe that Bitcoin offers no utility beyond serving as a ponzi scheme or a device for money laundering, then it would only be logical to conclude that consuming any amount of energy is wasteful. If you are one of the tens of millions of individuals worldwide using it as a tool to escape monetary repression, inflation, or capital controls, you most likely think that the energy is extremely well spent. Whether you feel Bitcoin has a valid claim on society's resources boils down to how much value you think Bitcoin creates for society.

Most energy production is geographically dependent, and usage is relatively inflexible. This means that power plants need to be located relatively close to the users of power since substantial loss occurs with the transmission of electricity over long distances. User demand is also relatively uncontrollable. When it's hot, people run air conditioners; when it's cold, they turn on the heat; and when it's dark, they turn on the lights. Because of this, systems need to be built to serve periods of peak demand. Most people would probably frown on having their heat cut off because it is using too much electricity at a certain time. What is unique about Bitcoin mining is that it is neither geographically dependent nor is the demand inflexible.

Bitcoin mining computers can be located anywhere. They can run on the methane gas from oil wells that is normally burned off and wasted. They can be placed near wind and solar farms to use any excess power generated beyond demand. They can be placed in remote areas to use otherwise unusable hydropower. They can also be turned off during periods of peak demand on the grid. This alternate view of Bitcoin's energy usage and potential is becoming more widely appreciated. For example, a *Forbes* article by Sam Lyman from September 21, 2023, titled "Why Bitcoin Mining Might Actually Be Great for Sustainability" states:

> In a recently published report, KPMG makes the case that bitcoin can serve a number of ESG functions—from stabilizing power grids and driving investment in renewables to monetizing stranded energy and capturing methane. The paper coincides with new research from Cambridge University and Bloomberg Intelligence that reveals bitcoin's environmental impact to be much smaller than previously thought...
>
> Matching supply with demand is one of the most significant challenges facing power providers. Too much energy production can overwhelm the grid. But so can too much demand. This is where bitcoin comes in.
>
> Bitcoin miners can act as an energy sponge, soaking up excess energy when needed to prevent it from overloading the grid. But they can just as easily shut off at a moment's notice when demand grows too high, as bitcoin miners did during a heat wave in Texas last month. The ability of bitcoin miners to do everything—or nothing—all at once is a boon to power providers. But it can also benefit customers by mitigating demand spikes to help keep prices low...

Bitcoin miners can tap into any energy source, anytime, anywhere in the world. And they are in constant search of low-cost energy, which they increasingly find in under-utilized renewable sources, such as hydro, wind, geothermal, and solar.

Because they are subject to the whims of nature, windmills, solar panels, and dams often create energy when nobody needs it. This is known as "stranded energy," and without a buyer, it goes to waste. Bitcoin, however, creates a robust marketplace for this kind of energy. Because the Bitcoin network runs 24/7/365, it can make use of renewable energy at all hours of the day and during any season of the year. Bitcoin's flexible demand load not only can increase revenue for green power providers but can also encourage further investment in clean energy.

A May 3, 2022, Bloomberg opinion piece by Trung Phan titled "Methane Is a Big Climate Problem That Bitcoin Can Help Solve" asserted: "The digital currency consumes a lot of electricity, but one startup is showing how its unique properties can help transition the world to cleaner energy."

A May 21, 2021, Reuters article by Laila Kearney titled "Insight: Oil Drillers and Bitcoin Miners Bond over Natural Gas" reported:

Extracting the currency from cyberspace, however, requires vast amounts of often-expensive electricity. Supercomputers must run constantly in a race against other "miners" to solve complex math problems in order to unlock digital vaults holding the currency. Placed in mobile trailers, these super-computers run as hot as 160 degrees Fahrenheit (71 degrees Celsius), and in the cold of western North Dakota, people stay warm just by sitting near them, cryptocurrency miners say.

The miners are increasingly sending these rigs out to oil fields because it's one of the cheapest ways to obtain the energy they need. Oil and natural gas come from the same wells, but at these sites, drillers are seeking crude oil and have no pipelines to get the gas to market. That typically forces them to burn it off in a process called flaring—creating carbon dioxide emissions—or to vent it into the atmosphere directly as methane.

"The sweet spot for us is stranded, low volumes of gas that don't justify a pipeline," said Steve Degenfelder, land manager at Wyoming-based producer Kirkwood Oil and Gas LLC, which has formed an alliance with Bitcoin miners.

Oil companies face pressure from investors and government officials to reduce emissions that lead to global warming. Sometimes they give the gas away for free to cryptocurrency miners; other times they sell it.

The National Hydropower Association in the United States has an article on its website, "Why Hydropower Owners Need to Talk with Bitcoin Miners," which says:

Bitcoin mining operations can help hydroelectric plants manage energy demand by utilizing excess electricity during periods of low demand.

During times when the electricity demand is low, such as during off-peak hours or during seasonal changes, hydroelectric plants can divert some of the excess electricity to power Bitcoin mining operations. This can help plants manage their electricity generation and reduce the wear and tear on generation units or wastage of excess electricity, which can result in lost revenue.

While Bitcoin clearly requires significant electricity, because miners seek the lowest-cost electricity and are not geographically restricted, they can go where the cheap or wasted power is. And because the mining computers can be turned on or off as required by peak demand or fluctuations in energy production, they are unique and useful energy users to help producers and grid operators.

Turns out that the *Newsweek* headline that Bitcoin would consume all the world's energy by 2020 was dead wrong.

BITCOIN AND SUSTAINABLE DEVELOPMENT IN THE GLOBAL SOUTH

An area widely overlooked by mainstream media is the contribution Bitcoin mining can make to expanding access to electricity. In some areas of the world, notably many areas of Africa, the electricity infrastructure is undeveloped, and it is economically difficult to bring power to many rural areas.

Abubakar Nur Khalil, a Nigerian Bitcoiner and CEO of Recursive Capital, noted in a May 24, 2024, *Forbes* article, "Africans Are Pioneering the Bright, Yet Complicated, Green Future of Bitcoin Mining":

> More than 500 million people in Africa currently lack reliable electricity access, according to the International Energy Agency. As such, one of Africa's most effective bitcoin mining strategies is to build micro grids powered by renewable energy sources in rural communities beyond the reach of main power grids.
>
> The Kenyan bitcoin mining company Gridless uses similar hydro-powered micro grids (under 1 megawatt capacity) to provide electricity to three rural communities in East Africa.

In May 2024, publicly traded US Bitcoin mining company Marathon Digital Holdings entered into an agreement with the government of Kenya with the objective "to support the utilization of energy and to optimize renewable energy projects across the Republic of Kenya." Chief executive officer Fred Thiel said the effort will focus on "monetizing underutilized energy across Kenya and jointly developing technology projects." Under the agreement, Marathon and Kenyan policymakers will cooperate to "better understand how to optimize renewable energy projects that produce surplus energy due to intermittency and seasonal variations," the press release said.

Les Novak discussed Bitcoin mining's impact on Africa in a post on Medium ("Harnessing Africa's Energy Transition: Bitcoin Mining as a Catalyst," May 11, 2024) and concluded:

> Africa stands at a crossroads in its journey towards energy transition. Bitcoin mining, despite its controversies, offers a unique opportunity to accelerate this transition while unlocking economic potential. By leveraging abundant renewable energy resources and embracing blockchain technology, African countries can chart a sustainable path towards universal energy access and economic prosperity. As the world watches, Africa has the chance to lead the way in shaping the future of energy and finance for generations to come.

A "Blueprint for Bitcoin Mining and Energy in Africa" (2023) from Bitcoin mining company Gridless suggests:

> Combining small-scale bitcoin data centers and renewables-based minigrids forms the foundation of a new model to expand profitable electrification to communities in emerging

MONEY, LOVE, AND BITCOIN

markets without the need for charity, aid, gifts, or government subsidy. The main challenge is that minigrids have a
low ROI [return on investment] and are not economically
viable without subsidies due to their high CAPEX cost, low
initial consumption, and long payback period.

The co-location of small-scale Bitcoin mining and
renewables-based microgrids helps to address the problem
of stranded renewable energy. By providing a consistent and
reliable demand for electricity, Bitcoin mining helps to utilize
excess renewable energy that might otherwise go to waste,
thereby unlocking the potential of stranded renewable energy
projects and contributing to a more sustainable energy future.

Michael Tobin and Ian Birrell describe a fascinating and
life-changing project in "The African Village Mining Bitcoin,"
on UnHerd, dated January 5, 2022, about Malawi:

Bondo is a scattered cluster of villages in a remote region
of Malawi near the border with Mozambique. It sits in the
foothills of Mount Mulanje, where residents rely on their
feet for transport and a few crops to feed their families. Yet
unlike in most places in this impoverished country, when
night descends they can now switch on lights, stoves and
televisions in their homes.

For electricity has arrived in Bondo. Three turbines
were installed in a micro-hydro scheme exploiting the fertile
region's rainfall. And the impact has been life-changing for
the 1,800 homes so far connected to a mini-grid. Children
can study after dark, so now have a better chance of passing
the exams for secondary school rather than having to leave
aged 11. Drugs and food can be stored in fridges, so villagers

do not have to make the 12-mile trek to the hospital and can produce batches of food or drinks to sell at market. Cooking the evening meal is three times quicker—and far less destructive to the environment—without the need to collect firewood.

Yet the big surprise in Bondo is not simply the supply of energy to such an isolated community, in a country where only one in eight citizens has access to grid electricity and on a continent where almost half the 1.2 billion population still lack this life-changing supply. The real eye-opener is the stack of 32 computers inside the concrete pump shed. This innovative mini-grid—located more than two hours from Malawi's second city of Blantyre along bumpy roads and tracks that can become impassable in a torrential downpour—is mining Bitcoin to fund its operation.

It is a smart idea. The computers used to create valuable new Bitcoin tokens and validate transactions consume around the same amount of energy as a medium-sized country such as Sweden would generate. Hence the stinging critique of how this cryptocurrency wastes the planet's precious resources. This initiative flips that narrative by using Bitcoin mining to fund energy in parts of Africa that are too poor or remote to merit connection to grids, but which do have plentiful supplies of potential power sources. Mining soaks up the excess energy of these renewable plants. And this delivers not just electricity but a powerful jolt to drive development in the local economy.

It is becoming clearer that Bitcoin mining may actually be a leading contributor to the viability of renewable and sustainable energy sources and a potential solution for some of the most vexing challenges in bringing the benefits of electricity to many areas where it has previously been uneconomic.

While there is no disputing that Bitcoin uses considerable electricity, it's just as important to dismiss the falsehoods and discern the truth behind its usage.

THE TRADITIONAL METHOD OF DEBT-BASED "HELPING"

The above examples of how Bitcoin mining can support the development of and access to sustainable energy stand in sharp contrast to the debt method of "helping" countries, particularly in the Global South. Bitcoin use and development in Africa, for example, offers tremendous opportunities for homegrown solutions to the needs of local communities. Africa has suffered under the tremendous weight of corrupted political and monetary systems and Bitcoin offers a new way out. There are many energetic, brilliant, and devoted African Bitcoiners who are doing some extraordinary work to solve many problems on the continent. Locally developed solutions stand in stark contrast to imposed systems. Great things are possible when we work together to support rather than exploit one another.

Unfortunately, the exploitation model has been used for many decades. In his *New York Times* bestselling book *Confessions of an Economic Hitman*, John Perkins describes a process in which the United States and other international organizations "help" countries develop their economies, build infrastructure, and increase GDP by designing major projects and supplying loans to these countries to implement them. This model was created when the traditional method of influence through military action became untenable in the nuclear age.

Wildly optimistic projections (along with outright threats)

are used to convince countries to take out large loans from the World Bank. The projects are then built by major Western engineering and construction firms that profit from their construction. While some of these projects may aid the country's economic development (though they primarily benefit the elite), many only result in excessive debt burdens beyond the country's ability to repay. They are then refinanced with new loans, perpetuating the debt cycle and resulting in further control by the perpetrators.

Perkins also asserts that these loans and refinance packages often come with strings attached that benefit the desires and interests of the governments backing the loans—for example, agreements allowing the installation of military bases. While critics dispute some of his claims, the history of major Western-backed development projects worldwide demonstrates the validity of his critique. A brief look at many of these projects reveals that they often don't turn out as planned and can't be paid for as expected. Even the United Nations secretary-general António Guterres has criticized these programs. A June 17, 2023, Associated Press article by Edith M. Lederer reports:

> From the ashes of World War II, three institutions were created as linchpins of a new global order. Now, in an unusual move, the top official in one—the secretary-general of the United Nations—is pressing for major changes in the other two.
>
> Antonio Guterres says the International Monetary Fund has benefited rich countries instead of poor ones. And he describes the IMF and World Bank's response to the COVID-19 pandemic as a "glaring failure" that left dozens of countries deeply indebted.

Guterres said it's time for the boards of the IMF and the World Bank to right what he called the historic wrongs and "bias and injustice built into the current international financial architecture."

That "architecture" was established when many developing countries were still under colonial rule.

Such schemes don't originate only in Western countries. In the 2023 third edition of his book, Perkins describes a playbook, only slightly different, being used by China with regard to its massive Belt and Road Initiative (BRI). Countries borrow from China to develop the BRI infrastructure allowing China to assert its influence in many areas of Africa and Central Asia. Whether it's the US or China, the effect of this approach wreaks havoc on the target countries and our planet as a whole.

Of course, buying influence by making loans that often benefit the lender more than the borrower is not a new phenomenon. However, the consequences of such are growing as more countries become indebted to the most powerful and influential nations. Extending influence in this manner generates deep resentment and anger as people, resources, and the environment are exploited.

Perkins says in *New Confessions of an Economic Hitman*, the second edition of his book:

> This book was written so that we may take heed and remold our story. I am certain that when enough of us become aware of how we are being exploited by the economic engine that creates an insatiable appetite for the world's resources, and results in systems that foster slavery, we will no longer tolerate it. We will reassess our role in a world where a few swim in

riches and the majority drown in poverty, pollution, and violence. We will commit ourselves to navigating a course toward compassion, democracy, and social justice for all.

These are worthy goals and ones I share.

9

Money is Not the Root

He that is of the opinion money will do everything may well be suspected of doing everything for money.

—BENJAMIN FRANKLIN

IT'S A BIT IRONIC that Franklin said this, as we will see in chapter 19. Yet, the point is clear. Whether we heard it quoted in the Pink Floyd song "Money" or elsewhere, we've probably all heard the saying: "Money is the root of all evil." Many of us may have also heard the more accurate version of this statement from the Bible: "The love of money is the root of all evil."

Most of us have known and experienced people who focused

solely on money, regardless of the impact of their actions on others. This gives the saying a ring of truth. But when we dig deeper, as I've explained, we realize money itself is just a technology used to store or convey the energy expended to create actual or perceived value. As philosopher and semanticist Alfred Korzybski said, "The map is not the territory." And similarly, the signal is not the message. No one loves a piece of paper or a bank statement. We love what we believe money can provide us, such as material goods, security, comfort, status, and power.

Money is not at the root. Money is more like the flowing sap of a tree, which transports the work product of the roots—water and nutrients—from the soil to the branches and leaves. Real money, like sap, is the result of actual transformative work being done. You can print and bury all the paper bills you want in your backyard, but that isn't what makes a tree grow, a flower blossom, or humanity better off.

VALUE OF WORK

Real money is not the same as the energy used to create value; it's just a way to keep track of it. So, the more value you add, the more money you earn. When you put in a lot of effort, whether physical, creative, or intellectual, to create value and make people's lives better, we acknowledge that and exchange our stored energy (money) to enjoy those benefits. In an ideal system, those who create more value accumulate more wealth. Why label what "transports" value creation, like sap, as the "root of evil"?

When money gets separated from the value of work, corrupted, or used as a tool of power, its dynamics get distorted. A king who uses the power of an army to extract wealth from citizens for his own enrichment and pleasure distorts the purer relationship between productive effort and reward. The people near the king who extract wealth from the citizenry by currying the king's favor and gaining largesse from the state also distort this relationship. The bankers and lenders who are close to the king and are granted exclusive charters, allowing them to control money and lending and to extort high fees, are rarely magnanimous actors. Is it any wonder that money has become associated with evil?

The origin of this phrase comes from the Christian tradition, where the apostle Paul, in his first letter to his young disciple Timothy, said: "For the love of money is a root of all kinds of evil. Some people, eager for money, have wandered from the faith and pierced themselves with many griefs" (1 Timothy 6:10).

The key concept left out of the shortened aphorism is "have wandered from the faith." Rather than interpreting the word "faith" as a religious doctrine or creed, suppose we consider faith in this context to mean acts of service, labor, or proof of work that add value for others. When we wander from the path of really adding value and merely seek to accumulate wealth, then we run into all sorts of troubles. The deeper wandering in this life is not about accumulating things but about better understanding the meaning of our lives and our place in the universe.

THE PURSUIT OF MONEY

The "evil" is not "in" money but is in the pursuit of money that is not tied to actual expenditures of energy to create real value and benefit to others. In fact, when someone contributes tremendous value and service to others, their resulting accumulation of wealth is a testament to the merits of their labor.

Whether someone contributes to meeting others' basic needs of food, shelter, and clothing or to the arts, architecture, science, philosophy, or spirituality, humanity is elevated. From this vantage, we can wander down the deeper paths of seeking greater understanding and awareness of the meaning of life.

We can all have differences in how we value products, services, works of art, music, and so on. The different values each of us ascribe to things reflect what we are willing to pay for them. One person may value fine art, another music, another flowers, and another clothes. Some may value clothes simply for protection from the elements, while others may value them for the fashion statement they make. Certain people might be willing to pay a fortune for something that others could care less about. This, in essence, is the process of price discovery, whereby the value people assign to goods is reflected in price. Where the rub comes in is if systems are in place that provide for the accumulation of wealth that is unconnected or disproportionate to the value offered.

We go astray when we see the marketplace as the primary indicator of value. Economic man acting in the marketplace for the consumption of goods to maintain life is a necessary and important function. But when the consumption of goods becomes the primary activity of life, we are missing more profound and deeper elements of life. Value is not the same as having a price in the marketplace. As Hannah Arendt noted in *The Human Condition*, "The much deplored devaluation of all things, that is, the loss of all intrinsic worth, begins with their transformation into values or commodities." We moved, she says, to a "society which replaced conspicuous production and its pride with 'conspicuous consumption' and its vanity."

VALUE REFLECTS CONSCIOUSNESS

In their book *Bitcoin is Venice*, Allen Farrington and Sacha Meyers discuss Carl Menger's *Principles in Economics* regarding price and value. Menger holds that the value of goods is not inherent but rather dependent upon people's judgment. Ultimately, Menger says, "Value does not exist outside the consciousness of man."

So, let's take this a step further. Isn't consciousness the ultimate value for humanity? Consciousness is what allows us to experience and explore what we value in life, the universe, and everything. While our values are reflected in economics, it is a representation and not the source. Consciousness is the source of our ascription of value to matter and life as well as of the desire to become more self-aware or, as Abraham Maslow calls it, "self-actualized."

Where or to what we ascribe value reflects our consciousness. If we ascribe value primarily to consumer products and consumption or to obtaining more units of society's currency, we will take actions that we believe will manifest these goals. Our focus will not be on what value we are contributing but on what we can extract. You become a taker, not a giver.

In his hierarchy of needs, Maslow suggests that base needs, such as food, water, air, clothing, and sleep, must be addressed first. Next, most people need to feel a sense of safety before they can focus on love and belonging. At the top of Maslow's pyramid is self-actualization, which is the need for morality, creativity, purpose, meaning, and transcendence.

It is hard to focus on purpose and meaning if you do not feel safe. As a teacher of mine in India says, "If a person is hungry, do not talk to them of consciousness and enlightenment. Feed them!" Some great souls, such as monks and spiritual masters, may care little about food, shelter, or clothing because they are focused primarily on the spiritual realms. These individuals, though, are few and far between.

I WANT MORE

On the other hand, many people never seem to be satisfied with what fills their bellies and so never seek to fill their hearts. In Hayao Miyazaki's film masterpiece, *Spirited Away*, Chihiro and her parents are moving to a new house. They get lost and find themselves in a new and exotic place. When Chihiro's parents come upon a restaurant and are offered endless delicacies in great abundance, they sit and start gorging themselves. Never leaving the feeding trough, they literally turn into pigs!

Chihiro is left alone while her parents eat, and she starts to explore this new world. She embarks on a twisting and turning journey (a hero's journey, as I will discuss later) to probe deeper into this fantastical world. She glimpses love in the form of a boy and pursues understanding who he and she really are. Though obstacles are at every turn, only a deeper understanding of life and love will satisfy her.

Everyone is on their own journey, yet we can become unbalanced in a culture and society that focuses relentlessly on an ever-expanding list of "safety" needs. There seems to be a never-ending list of things the marketers tell us we need to be happy. Have you ever gotten that thing you wanted so badly, only to have it replaced with yet another thing you must have? So many people in the world are pursuing money to get more things that don't, in the end, really satisfy them. There's nothing wrong with having a Lamborghini, but having a fleet of them will not bring enlightenment.

We "wander from the faith" and never ascend to higher levels of awareness or consciousness when we only focus on the stuff we want. On the other hand, as my teacher pointed out, many people can barely satisfy their basic needs. Corrupted systems have often extracted so much from them that there is little left to sustain life.

Wall Street has created an endless supply of financial products for the sole purpose of generating more money. Fire and life insurance provide a community service by sharing risk and providing some protection from catastrophes. Credit default swaps, on the other hand, are just a financial shell game of covering debt with wrapping paper. They are pretty much just what Dickens described in the quote in chapter 7. While some financial structures can provide value by making markets, providing access to investment capital, or providing stores of value, many operations extract money (fees) while providing little value. Computing capacity and technology allow for algorithmic high-frequency trading, but it's hard to see what the value is other than for the traders who extract money from the system.

In the great 1948 film noir classic *Key Largo*, a group of people are being held hostage in a Florida Keys hotel by gangsters as they ride out a hurricane. Humphrey Bogart's character, Frank McCloud, says that what makes the gangster Johnny Rocco (played by Edward G. Robinson) special is he knows what he wants. Rocco stutters when asked to describe what he wants, only for McCloud to fill in, "He wants more." To which Rocco answers, "Yeah, that's it. More. That's right. I want more." When asked, "Will you ever get enough?" Rocco replies, "Well, I never have. No, I guess I won't." Rocco asks McCloud, "Do you know what you want?" He responds, "Yes, I had hopes once, but I gave them up." "Hopes for what?" Rocco asks, and McCloud replies, "A world in which there's no place for Johnny Rocco." I'm with Bogart's character on this one, but I haven't given up.

GOVERNMENT WANDERINGS

When systems are abused, and people siphon resources rather than contribute value, prices become distorted, and savings mechanisms are corrupted. Real investment means using money (capital) to generate and create greater value. For example, investing in education gives you more skills to contribute to society. When markets are distorted through artificial interest rates, tax policies, or government favoritism, money is wasted on projects for financial gain, not for making useful things.

Tax policies are also often wielded as a tool to boost certain activities that a free market might not naturally endorse. Consequently, investment money is directed toward these projects primarily to reap the associated tax benefits. In some cases, these endeavors serve socially beneficial purposes that the government, acting on behalf of its citizens, wishes to encourage. In many instances, however, lobbyists leverage their influence to convince lawmakers to offer tax incentives favoring specific industries or projects. As a result, investment flows into these endeavors—not because they are inherently sound projects—so that subpar projects are funded and valuable resources end up squandered.

Similarly, artificially suppressed interest rates allow large financial institutions to borrow money at very low costs and then invest these funds in projects that otherwise might not make good investments. If the financial institution gets in trouble, the government ends up bailing it out anyway. A moral hazard is created when government institutions step in and prevent the adverse consequences of bad decisions by any entity or industry.

In many countries, crony capitalism or crony socialist systems are the norm. Politicians ensure that governments favor the entities that support them and keep them in power. Governments have legitimate purposes that can serve the common interest, but when policies and activities go beyond those that truly serve the citizenry, grave problems are created.

A state provides certain benefits to its citizens for which we assign a value and so are willing to pay taxes. People protest and object when their taxes go to pay for activities they do not see as adding value. While opinions differ on the government's role, the principle is what is relevant. In democracies, there is a feeling that at least we have a say (a vote) in the actions and priorities of the state. When mechanisms of the state leave people feeling they have little or no say in what happens and much that occurs is for the sake of enriching politicians and their cronies, tensions and distrust arise.

The feeling that our state has "wandered from the faith" and drifted from what the people consented to begins to take hold. Couple this with an increase in wealth inequality, and the flames of discontent are further fanned. Populism arises to give voice to anger and frustration. Politicians respond to this anger by providing simple, but usually erroneous, answers as to the source of and solution to any problem. All the while, the populace still senses they are primarily pawns in a system that accrues the most power and money to politicians and industrialists and those most connected to them.

A Brookings Institute report from May 16, 2023, authored by Zia Qureshi, "Rising Inequality: A Major Issue of Our Time," begins with this summary:

Income and wealth inequality has risen in many countries in recent decades. Rising inequality and related disparities and anxieties have been stoking social discontent and are a major driver of the increased political polarization and populist nationalism that are so evident today. An increasingly unequal society can weaken trust in public institutions and undermine democratic governance. Mounting global disparities can imperil geopolitical stability.

This was evidenced in the "Great Financial Crisis," during which governments bailed out large financial institutions while many ordinary homeowners lost their homes. Frustration and disgust at this crony capitalism further undermined confidence in our system.

In response to the COVID-19 pandemic, governments handed out small checks to the populace who were unable to work and large checks to corporations and financial institutions to keep the lubrication of money flowing. Yet the money distributed was not from the coffers of tax collection—the real wealth of the citizenry who generates it—but from the power of seigniorage—the ability of a government to create money without the endorsement of an informed public. As we have seen, when money isn't tied to the real effort that creates value, the value of money decreases. Inflation is the degradation in the purchasing power of a currency. It ends up as an insidious tax on those least able to afford it.

THE EVIL IS IN THE MANIPULATION

A now famous statement of clarity and candor occurred when CBS correspondent Scott Pelley interviewed Federal Reserve chairman Jerome Powell for an episode of *60 Minutes* that aired Sunday, May 17, 2020, in the wake of the government's response to the COVID-19 pandemic.

In the interview, Powell made clear how the Federal Reserve manipulates the supply of money in the economy.

PELLEY: Fair to say you simply flooded the system with money?

POWELL: Yes. We did. That's another way to think about it. We did.

PELLEY: Where does it come from? Do you just print it?

POWELL: We print it digitally. So as a central bank, we have the ability to create money digitally. And we do that by buying Treasury Bills or bonds or other government guaranteed securities. And that actually increases the money supply. We also print actual currency and we distribute that through the Federal Reserve banks.

If money is supposed to represent something of real value, something that results from bona fide effort to produce products and services of value from our precious time and labor, how can the Federal Reserve just print it without it compromising the value and integrity of the currency and the labor it is supposed to represent?

But it's even worse than that because the "benefits" of this additional money in the system are unequally distributed. The Cantillon effect is the principle that those closest to the money printer and who have first access to the money can capitalize by buying assets before any price increases resulting from the inflationary effect of a money supply increase (as discussed in chapter 2). Those without access must wait for the money to trickle down to them, by which time prices have risen. When the Fed prints money, they don't credit our accounts with the new money. It goes to the reserve accounts of major financial institutions.

Axel Weber, a fellow at the Foundation for Economic Education, in an article, "Inflation Not Only Hurts, It Diverts," puts it this way:

> When the state expands the credit and money supply, it redistributes purchasing power and causes the misallocation of resources in the market. In that redistribution, there are necessarily winners who are able to purchase more and losers who are able to purchase less. This is called the Cantillon effect, named after Richard Cantillon (1680-1734) who first observed that money creation has uneven effects in the market.
>
> When the state prints and spends money or makes money available to lenders, the government and the early recipients of the new money benefit. But that gain necessarily comes at the expense of others, because the new money has not produced any additional real wealth...
>
> The way money is created is of the utmost importance, for the original recipients of money benefit the most. Clearly, businesses have an incentive to be close to the money spigot to maximize their benefits and minimize their losses. The logical conclusion of this fact is that the Fed can never operate as a neutral party, disinterestedly optimizing the market.
>
> Now it is clear that inflation is not only the devaluation of money that causes the prices of goods like Oreos to rise. It also redirects resources with some winners and losers,

and it allows the politicians' priorities to take precedence over individuals within the market. It's a dangerous tool that rewards the businesses that collude with the state at the expense of everyone else.

Money is not evil, but its manipulation through money printing and resulting inflation sure is. This is wandering from the faith. It is not the path of love. Those in the developed Western world, with currencies backed by large economies, armies, and manipulated systems, have benefited from this system. But, even for them, the foundational cracks are getting wider and deeper. Meanwhile, for those in many other countries without the power of a reserve currency or its cousins, the devaluation of money is making life increasingly difficult. In fact, in many countries, governments manipulate the money supply, leading to hyperinflation. With hyperinflation, wealth is destroyed even faster than it is created. There is no answer to hyperinflation without huge adverse impacts on society.

FIAT CURRENCY

Fiat currency is the term for money issued by governments that is not backed by gold or anything else. Fiat is a Latin word that means "let it be so." It is defined as an "arbitrary order or decree." Fiat currency is something that is created solely by the authority of the ruler or state. Hence, central banks around the world arbitrarily create money out of thin air based on their "authority."

Why do they do this? Well, wouldn't you create more money if you could? Counterfeiting is a crime unless the government is doing it! With more money, politicians can promise more government benefits and incentives to get votes and retain power.

The debt that is accumulated is not their debt but the citizens'.

At high debt levels, there is little chance that a growing economy or tax base will be enough to pay off the debt. The only way a country can avoid default is to print more money and take on more debt.

If a country has one hundred dollars in income from taxes and wants to spend one hundred dollars or more on public programs, but it also has one thousand dollars in debt requiring one hundred dollars in interest payments, where is the other hundred dollars going to come from? The only way to pay the debt without raising taxes or cutting benefits, services, or military spending is to create more money. When the government prints new money, one hundred dollars in this case, to pay the interest owed on the debt, the debtholders are getting their nominal dollar payment, but it is worth less in purchasing power. This is why inflation is a necessary and integral part of economies built on excessive levels of government spending and debt.

If we could pay our credit card bill or mortgage by creating money and passing it off as having the same value as the original debt incurred, it would be an understandable temptation. Yet, it is an action without integrity, and all actions have effects. As debtholders become more concerned with the chance of getting paid back with money of comparable value, they become less interested in making loans, so interest rates will rise (supply and demand again), and it will be harder to borrow money and stay afloat. When your credit card balance increases beyond your income to pay it, eventually, you get cut off.

While the average citizen may not be too concerned about wealthy bondholders, when the value of our money is reduced through money printing, we lose the value of our savings while prices rise. And, as we have recently experienced, when banks lose money because of changes in interest rates and bond values, governments and central bankers bail them out with even more money printing. This is the evil inflation tax that is imposed on those least able to afford it.

I am not ignoring the tremendous achievements and improvements that have occurred during (but not necessarily because of) the reign of fiat currencies. And we do not need to ascribe or debate malicious intent as regards what I have been describing (though there is plenty of evidence of it). I suggest that you look at the path we have been on, evaluate the pluses and minuses, and at least consider exploring a revolutionary new path that has been engineered for our new digital age.

Upon reflection, it is no wonder money seems to be the root of all evil. In many ways, our current system of money (and many of those that collapsed before it) has had tremendously deleterious effects on people if they are not close to the top of society. The fiat system may have had its benefits at one time when the technology it offered was an improvement over the physical transport of metals, but we have ventured from an analog to a new digital age. As we will explore in chapter 11, "The Path of Bitcoin," new paths are possible in this new age. Before that, though, let's turn to the laws of cause and effect.

10

The Karma of Money

How people treat you is their karma; how you react is yours.
—WAYNE W. DYER

TWO GROSSLY MISUNDERSTOOD IDEAS are money and karma. So, let's try to bring some light and understanding to the intersection of these two concepts.

As we've discussed, money is like everything else in the universe—it is a form of energy. Specifically, money is a technology for transferring or storing the energy associated with labor. You work, you get paid in money, and you can use that money to buy what you need or want. If you don't consume as much as the value of your labor, you can save the difference. That savings is capital. Capital is not an evil thing. It is simply stored money that can be put to future use or invested to try to create more value.

PAYCHECK TO PAYCHECK

As we know, much of the world lives paycheck to paycheck. This means that the money people earn from their labor is consumed for basic living expenses before the next paycheck comes in. There is little or no excess money to be saved; hence, most people cannot accumulate capital and, therefore, build wealth.

Living paycheck to paycheck has huge consequences for individuals, families, and society. When there is no financial cushion, people can have little sense of security. With no security, their level of anxiety goes up. And, when personal or economic disruptions occur (job loss, health issues, economic recessions, and inflation, among others) and there is no emergency fund, lives and families can be thrown into upheaval, and traumatic losses can occur. And, as noted by Mr. Ammous and many spiritual teachers, when people have to be focused on survival, there is little inclination to turn to the deeper meaning of life.

When someone consumes less than they earn, money can be saved. However, as I explained earlier, with no effective means of preserving the value of that money, there is a disincentive to saving, and consumption is encouraged. Without a store of value that protects the value of savings, then it is impossible to accumulate any level of wealth. Our current system encourages consumer spending and consumption to keep the economy moving rather than saving and capital accumulation.

HOW TO THINK OF KARMA

Now, let's look at karma. The meaning of karma has many layers and comes from ancient Indian Vedic texts. It's often thought of as some giant ledger book of good and bad deeds settled in some cosmic system of reward and punishment. Most people casually use the term to explain that misfortune, illness, or problems are due to a person having committed some error in the past, so the current problems represent some kind of payment for it to "even the score." This simplistic view misses the term's deeper meanings.

Karma is, in essence, action, and actions have effects. Humans label things "good" or "bad" and judge actions or people, but the laws of physics, energy, and karma just mean that actions have consequences. Our actions have effects, and the intention behind the action also matters.

MONETARY SYSTEMS HAVE CONSEQUENCES

So, what does this have to do with money? Well, the karma of money means that the actions we take with our labor and the money it results in will have effects. The same is true for the monetary systems of the societies we live in. Most people feel a sense of pride in "a job well done." We all tend to be aware of the difference between people whose work or actions earn them certain rewards and those who are given benefits that bear little relationship to their actions. Now, the reality is that most of us live in societies where everyone does not start off on a level playing field; their accumulated rewards may or may not be the result of their own actions, but they certainly are a consequence of many other actions.

A very real problem arises in society when systems are set up that don't allow people to save money effectively. In our current global financial system, big central banks create money without anyone putting in real work. They dish it out to governments (through bond purchases) and big financial institutions. When some entity can make money without working for it, it devalues the money that people earn through hard work and smart savings. This is called monetary inflation (as discussed in chapter 2), and it's like a sneaky "tax" that hits the folks furthest away from the largesse of the money printers.

The American Revolution kicked off partly because people were furious about "taxation without representation" by their British rulers. When the Federal Reserve makes money out of thin air, and the government spends money it doesn't have, expecting no outcomes of this is wishful thinking. It's like a magic trick by central bankers—it may look good for a while, but eventually, the illusion fades, and the consequences hit. We're seeing it now in rising prices for gas, food, and real estate, which is like a tax on everyone. Even though technology and productivity should be making things cheaper, monetary inflation keeps making everything more expensive!

Even one of the great industrialists of the last century, Henry Ford, knew that if the masses understood the organization of our financial system, it would not be tolerated. He understood how the system could be manipulated even long before the full reign of fiat monetary systems. It's summed up in this statement widely attributed to him: "It is well enough that people of the nation do not understand our banking and monetary system, for if they did, I believe there would be a revolution before tomorrow morning."

When, as a society, we don't see our monetary system for

what it is and fail to penetrate its illusions and deceptions in order to take appropriate action to correct it, there is no avoiding the effects of the karma (the actions) our monetary system and its manipulation create. Money has been used as a tool to wield power, influence, and control. When, as a society, we allow the perpetuation of a system of money creation that is divorced from the energy of value creation, we will all suffer the repercussions.

There are no easy answers or fixes to this karmic cycle that has been set in motion. And its effects will surely be felt by many. A Himalayan yoga master, Anand Mehrotra, once explained karma to me this way: Once an arrow is shot, it cannot be stopped. The action has been taken. And, if you are standing in its way, it will strike you, and you will be affected. Karma, however, can be transcended by someone if they step out of the way of the arrow. The action has been taken, the arrow has been shot, and effects will occur. The result may be injury if you are standing in its path, or you may not be struck if you move in time.

Consider this concept in the context of our interactions with others. If someone is hurling insults at you and you absorb the words as truth, you will be impacted. Suppose someone calls you ugly. When you stand in the path of this arrow and believe you are ugly, your self-worth and self-confidence may be affected. You might start feeling bad about yourself, and you might think you are not worthy of being loved and cherished as beautiful. Alternatively, you can step out of the arrow's path by realizing that the insult says more about that person than you. It is a reflection of their state, not yours. Your beauty is a reflection of you, not of someone else's problems. The deeper meaning of karma and its transcendence are valuable lessons.

DODGING ARROWS

OK, back to money. In our current global financial and monetary system, an entire quiver of arrows has been launched. Many around us may be hit, and many others will surely be grazed in some way. However, if we take action to move out of the way, the strikes may not be fatal.

We may feel we have little say or control over these launchers of monetary arrows, but we can respond. We have two choices: we can stand in the path and rail at them or simply step out of their way. By educating ourselves about how the system functions, we can decide whether to move onto a new path. But will that path be the one with the greatest potential to lead us to a more decentralized, honest, and equitable global financial system? Is it a good path or not?

11

The Path of Bitcoin

Any path is only a path, and there is no affront, to oneself or to others, in dropping it if that is what your heart tells you... Look at every path closely and deliberately. Try it as many times as you think necessary. Then ask yourself, and yourself alone, one question... Does this path have a heart? If it does, that path is good; if it doesn't, it is of no use.

— CARLOS CASTANEDA

FRITJOF CAPRA BEGINS HIS SEMINAL WORK, *The Tao of Physics*, with this quote from Castaneda's book, *The Teachings of Don Juan*. I first read Capra's book as a high school student before going on to study philosophy in college. Just before I had my aha moment, which propelled me down the Bitcoin path, I was in India as the COVID-19 pandemic broke. Having recently left my career as a Certified Financial Planner ® and wealth manager, I went to India for long-deferred additional yoga training. Coincidentally, one of the books my young teacher had made required reading was *The Tao of Physics*. He grinned wide and let out his joyful laugh when I told him, "I read that book before you were even born!"

In his book, Capra highlights the parallels between modern quantum physics and the insights gained through mystical exploration in various Eastern wisdom traditions. Quantum physics revolutionized classical Newtonian physics, challenging its mechanical laws and the idea of a solid atom as the fundamental building block of matter.

Capra quotes Albert Einstein from his autobiography, "All my attempts to adapt the theorctical foundation of physics to this (new type of) knowledge failed completely. It was as if the ground had been pulled out from under one, with no firm foundation to be seen anywhere, upon which one could have built."

IT MAKES NO SENSE

When physicists a hundred years ago began penetrating beyond classical physics' Newtonian mechanical laws, the results of their experiments and the discoveries made seemed to make no sense. It's kind of like how Bitcoin—"magic Internet money"—seems to make no sense. How often have you heard statements like these?

- It isn't backed by anything.
- Bitcoin is a Ponzi scheme.
- It's rat poison squared.
- It's a speculative bubble.
- It's bad for the environment.

- It's for terrorists and criminals.
- The government will ban it.

Most of us live in societies where there is little question about what money is. Money is something issued by governments. You can hold it, trade it for things, put it in the bank, and use it as "legal tender for all debts, public and private." If you live in the United States, your wallet contains the most coveted money on the planet, the US dollar. You may or may not believe in God, but we all know the power of a Benji.

So, when a group of cypherpunks comes along and suggests that some software code is money, most people would feel a bit like Einstein did when he attempted to adapt what he knew to a new type of knowledge, and it "failed completely." How could some software code be money? It "does not compute." You'd have to really be "lost in space" if you don't know what money is and think some bit of code that is not backed by a government, or even gold, could be money.

While we may not understand it, we've seen the power unleashed by theoretical physics' evolved understanding of matter in the form of the atom bomb, which evidenced the power of the energy contained in atomic matter. Quantum physics pushed humanity to question our previous level of knowledge. It forced us to go beyond our former level of understanding to a deeper one and have an appreciation of the powerful interactions among energetic forces, including the human actor and observer.

The salient point here is that some of the most revolutionary discoveries turned our previous understanding of things upside down. Humans have always striven to enhance our ability to navigate the forces in the universe. New discoveries and ideas often produce better methods or models not only for

understanding and interacting with each other but for comprehending the forces at the root of all life as well.

By delving into the secrets of nature and the universe, we
develop new systems and technologies to serve humankind.
Roman engineers built aqueducts that still stand today to deliver
water to cities and agricultural fields based on transformative
mechanical engineering principles. Architects and engineers of
antiquity erected massive temples, cathedrals, and monuments
that remain awe-inspiring today. We have propelled ourselves,
quite literally, through and into space with the development
of transportation technologies from cars, trains, and planes to
rocket ships. Through the clever use of materials, computer
chips shrink in size but grow in capacity.

Despite all the evidence of so much progress, it seems to
be human nature to resist new approaches. Remember Galileo,
who was imprisoned for the heretical idea that the earth revolved
around the sun? Just because something doesn't fit with our
current, familiar model doesn't mean it isn't true or useful.

CONSIDERING A NEW PROTOCOL

So, shouldn't we at least consider the possibility that a software
protocol could be a vastly improved and revolutionary form of
money? Most of us don't understand how a cell phone works,
yet, as an innovation, we know there is no comparing one to
an old copper-wired landline, rotary-dial phone. Dick Tracy's
1946 wristwatch phone was comic strip fiction until it wasn't.

The use of some technologies has been of tremendous value
to humanity, while others, perhaps, not so much. The attempts
at first flight resulted in some pretty ridiculous-looking contrap-
tions, but eventually, the right engineering was hit upon, so

humans left the ground and stayed up without crashing disastrously. The same is true for cryptocurrencies—some may be of great value and do the job right, and others may not.

When Bitcoin was launched, it was unknown if it really would take off. The Wright brothers had enough understanding of the issues involved to create a system that could propel humanity into the realm of the birds. In order to bring together solutions to many very complex issues, Bitcoin was launched as a best effort to propel money onto a new path. What many don't understand is that Bitcoin was developed on top of decades of technological and engineering progress in cryptography, security challenges, digital dilemmas, and protocol developments. Much of this was the product of government and military research.

There have been many copycat "cryptocurrencies." (Infamously, those with pictures of dogs on them.) Unlike Bitcoin, their conceptions were anything but immaculate. The crypto universe has been heavily polluted by those simply trying to make a quick buck, giving the term a bad name. We call them "shitcoins" because they are primarily scams to enrich their initial developers at the expense of the public. Most of these are so fundamentally different in their nature and intent from Bitcoin that Bitcoiners are clear—Bitcoin, not cryptocurrency.

Do not paint Bitcoin and other cryptocurrencies with the same broad brush. Instead, the salient point is to question, as per Castaneda: "Is Bitcoin a path with a heart?" Is it a path worthy of exploring and following? Why on earth does "heart" even matter when it comes to money? And, just what is love, and what does it have to do with Bitcoin?

12

What is Love?

When we love, we always strive to become better than we are. When we strive to become better than we are, everything around us becomes better too.

—PAULO COELHO

LOVE IS THE INSPIRATION FOR THIS BOOK, and yet, it can be challenging to discuss it meaningfully. Love is outside the domain of science and logic and facts and rationality. Describing it is more the realm of poets, authors, philosophers, and highly evolved masters. While at times we may have been confused about what love really is, most of us have probably had the experience of love because it is within us.

Love is not something out there. It is not something that we have to go find. We may wish to find someone to share our love with, but love is ultimately an inside job. If you want to know what love is (as the old Foreigner song pleaded), you've got to start with your own heart. Love resides within all of us. Expressing and sharing it is a profound experience. The term "love" is thrown around casually quite a lot. So, let's delve a little deeper into love and what some have said about it.

LOVE IS NOT A SIMPLE WORD

As anyone who has felt love knows, it is just something that is. It is not based on a logical analysis of various factors, it is not a function of checking all the boxes, and it is not the trifling sentiment of a greeting card. Love is not bondage; love is freeing.

Author Margaret Atwood said, "The Eskimo has fifty-two names for snow because it is important to them; there ought to be as many for love." And yet, we use one catchall term (at least in the English language) to cover the most important of all things in life and its different characteristics and layers. Romantic love between two intimate partners is different from a mother's love for her child. Expressing love through your work is not how you show love for your football team. Loving chocolate is different from loving to garden. Showing love for your father will not be how you show love for a teammate. We undoubtedly could, as Atwood suggests, come up with fifty-two names for these different types of love, but what informs all such expressions? So, is love a transient and fleeting emotion linked merely to circumstances, hormones, or needs? Or is it something fundamentally deeper?

WHAT LOVE IS NOT

We also know plenty of things that sure don't look, act, or feel like love. We see and experience anger, fear, resentment, hatred, mistrust, dishonesty, and at least fifty more adjectives and verbs for human feelings, emotions, and actions that don't feel or look like love. We form attachments to people, objects, or emotions, and when we fear their loss, we often respond with unloving actions. As Swami Rama wrote in his book *Living with the Himalayan Masters*:

> Many people confuse attachment with love. But in attach-
> ment you become selfish, interested in your own pleasure,
> and you misuse love. You become possessive and try to gain
> the objects of your desires. Attachment creates bondage while
> love bestows freedom.

Feeling and experiencing love in a world filled with war, poverty, starvation, injustice, and inequity is not always an easy task. Yet, in any circumstance, anywhere and anyplace, we can experience love.

Quantum physics shows us that just because an object looks solid to our organs of perception does not mean that it really is. The fact that fear and unloving actions exist does not mean love isn't present either. Humans might act in ways that don't look like love, even when the motivation behind such actions might be. Conflicts, for example, can occur when we fear for the safety of those we love. The desire to protect them can cause us to act in a manner that may not seem like love. Humans with limited perspectives on love, coupled with undeveloped skills in communication and conflict resolution, can act in seemingly unloving ways. The misguided strategies we employ may not look like love, but the motivations underlying them may be.

CONDITIONED PROGRAMMING

We all have software bugs—unconscious triggers—that set off emotions that result in actions that don't seem very loving. The reptilian part of our brains operates on fight-or-flight reactions. Its modus operandi is looking for and identifying threats. Sometimes, it does that accurately, and sometimes, it wholly misidentifies them.

Some of what the subconscious mind determines as a threat arises from unmet needs stored as internal trauma during infancy and the early childhood development years. These contribute to someone identifying the world as a threatening and unloving place, and fear becomes their default reaction. And actions from fear rarely show up looking like expressions of love. Generational trauma within cultures or families adds another layer of disturbance and pain that is often poorly appreciated or understood.

When the reptilian and limbic parts of the brain perceive threats and generate a fear response or the subconscious mind is running conditioned programs, causing us to believe we are threatened, it's not easy to switch to a more conscious program to determine if the threat is real and respond wisely. As Bruce Lipton, a stem cell biologist and an internationally recognized leader in bridging science and spirit, in his book, *The Biology of Belief,* says:

> The subconscious mind is primarily a repository of stimulus-response tapes derived from instincts and learned experiences. The subconscious mind is fundamentally habitual; it will play the same behavioral responses to life's signals over and

over again…When it comes to sheer neurological processing abilities, the subconscious mind is more than a million times more powerful than the conscious mind.

This is a very useful function. It allows us to do all sorts of daily (often highly complex tasks) without "thinking" about them. It's what allows us to drive a car to work on automatic pilot. But when these default programs are emotional or trauma-based, it takes effort not only to override them but to rewrite them. As a result, much of humanity runs on subconscious programs loaded into us in childhood, sometimes not by the best programmers!

LOVING FROM THE CONSCIOUS MIND

The prefrontal cortex, the seat of consciousness, operates differently. Lipton continues:

> The conscious mind—which represents the seat of our personal identity, source, or spirit—is the creative mind. It can see into the future, review the past, or disconnect from the present moment as it solves problems in our head. In its creative capacity, the conscious mind holds our wishes, desires, and aspirations for our lives.

The conscious mind allows us to tune in to higher frequencies and be more self-reflective, aware, and loving. Depending on the quality of our commitment to engaging in evolving and self-reflection, we will grow and evolve our own awareness and love. "You can live a life of fear or live a life of love. You have the choice!" Lipton declares.

But is this really a choice, or are humans by their very nature a violent species? The fact that violence exists does not mean that it must exist or that it is an inherent and unchangeable characteristic of the human species. Lipton says:

> Most human violence is neither necessary nor is it an inherent, genetic, "animal" survival skill. We have the ability, and I believe the evolutionary mandate, to stop violence. The best way to stop it is to realize...that we are spiritual beings who need love as much as we need food. But we won't get to the next evolutionary step by just thinking about it...Survival of the Most Loving is the only ethic that will ensure not only a healthy personal life, but also a healthy planet.

To rephrase Henry Ford's famous aphorism a bit: if we think we can, or we think we can't create more loving relationships and a more loving world, we will be right.

THE CHARACTERISTICS OF LOVE

Poets, philosophers, and spiritual teachers help us reflect on and tune in to the true nature of love. So, let's turn to see what some of them have said about love, fear, and their respective characteristics.

Don Miguel Ruiz, in *The Mastery of Love*, writes:

> Every human being has a personal dream of life and that dream is completely different from anyone else's dream... Just as your body is made of cells, your dreams are made by emotions. There are two main sources of those emotions: One is fear, and all the emotions that come from fear; the

other is love, and all the emotions that come from love. We experience both emotions, but the one that predominates in everyday people is fear.

He goes on to describe the characteristics of love compared to fear:

- Love has no obligations. Fear is full of obligations.

- Love has no expectations. Fear is full of expectations.

- Love is based on respect, but fear doesn't respect anything, including itself.

- Love is ruthless; it doesn't feel sorry for anyone, but it does have compassion. Fear is full of pity; it feels sorry for everyone.

- Love is completely responsible. Fear avoids responsibility, but this doesn't mean that it's not responsible.

- Love is always kind. Fear is always unkind.

- Anger is nothing but fear with a mask.

- Love is unconditional. Fear is full of conditions.

Thich Nhat Hanh, a Vietnamese Buddhist monk, described true love as follows:

True love is made of four elements: kindness, compassion, joy, and equanimity. If your love contains these elements, it will be healing and transforming, and it will have the element of holiness in it. True love has the power to heal and transform any situation and bring deep meaning to our lives.

I'll close this chapter with musings on love from various poets, teachers, songwriters, and spiritual leaders.

"Your heart knows the way. Run in that direction." — **RUMI**

"Love possesses not nor would it be possessed; For love is sufficient unto love... And think not you can direct the course of love, for love, if it finds you worthy, directs your course. Love has no other desire but to fulfill itself." — **KHALIL GIBRAN**

"Love is the answer / And you know that for sure / Love is the flower / You gotta let it, you gotta let it grow." — **JOHN LENNON**

"Love is the bridge between you and everything." — **RUMI**

"Love: You're not meant to wait for it. You're not meant to search for it. You're meant to generate it." — **MICHAEL BECKWITH**

"Power is of two kinds. One is obtained by the fear of punishment and the other by acts of love. Power based on love is a thousand times more effective and permanent than the one derived from fear of punishment." — **MAHATMA GANDHI**

"Love is the affinity which links and draws together the elements of the world...Love, in fact, is the agent of universal synthesis." — **PIERRE TEILHARD DE CHARDIN**

"The important thing is not to think much, but to love much, and so to do what best awakens us to love." — **SAINT TERESA OF AVILA**

"That Love is all there is/Is all we know of Love" — **EMILY DICKINSON**

The more we operate from self-awareness, self-reflection, and a higher level of consciousness, the more we will act in and from a place of love. In the same way that choosing to lean into love rather than fear is a process of working to rewrite our default programs, deciding to reprogram our monetary system through better technology will be a process. Breaking free from the old programs of money and committing to a new paradigm and the systems to support it takes a leap of faith, just as crossing the bridge from fear to love does. Both are well worth it.

Just as through mindfulness we can direct our actions to come from a place of love, so, too, must we be mindful of the principles that should be the basis of a new monetary system. It might seem odd to keep bringing the topics of money and Bitcoin back to love, but if love is all there is...

13

What If Love is the Protocol?

The things best to know are first principles and causes, but these things are perhaps the most difficult for men to grasp, for they are farthest removed from the senses.

— ARISTOTLE, *METAPHYSICS*

BITCOIN IS A SOFTWARE PROTOCOL. It is a set of standards and rules that govern the operation of the Bitcoin system. As software code, it is a rules-based program in which the participants agree to follow the system's rules. It is based on first principles.

THE ORIGINS OF THE PROTOCOL

A look at the history of the word "protocol" is interesting. Merriam-Webster states the following:

> In Late Greek, the word *prōtokollon* referred to the first sheet of a papyrus roll bearing the date of its manufacture. In some instances, it consisted of a flyleaf that was glued to the outside of a manuscript's case and provided a description of its contents. Coming from the Greek prefix *prōto-* ("first") and the noun *kolla* ("glue"), *prōtokollon* gave us our word *protocol*.

Thus, a protocol is the first page in a document that binds it together and describes its contents. It is often used to refer to the official procedure or system of rules governing the operation of a system. In 2008, a person or entity referred to as Satoshi Nakamoto distributed a paper titled "Bitcoin: A Peer-to-Peer Electronic Cash System." This paper has come to be known as the "Bitcoin white paper." It is a brief but brilliant description of a system of rules, conventions, and codes of operation of a new monetary system. It is the summary protocol of first principles for what has become a global network of millions of participants and more than a trillion dollars of value.

One of the greatest accomplishments of the Bitcoin white paper and the core system it describes is the relative simplicity of the protocols. While they are sophisticated in that they solve extraordinarily difficult cryptographic problems, they are also relatively simple in principle and operation. Like anything, simple systems can have shortcomings, but due to their simplicity, they often avoid the potential compounding of problems associated with overcomplexity.

While there were early challenges to the Bitcoin protocols and efforts to change them, the code has remained essentially untouched over time. As more people adopt Bitcoin and more participants opt in to agreement with the protocols, changing the code becomes more difficult. After more than sixteen years, the protocols have stood the test of time. Minor technological improvements have been adopted, and systems to increase the efficiency of the network for smaller transactions (for example, the Lightning and Liquid networks) have been built on top ("layer 2") of the core protocols. The key takeaway is that the monetary policy of the Bitcoin network is not something that changes.

It's a different story in the United States, the European Union, and many countries with central banks, where monetary policy seems to change almost every month. Stock and bond markets are constantly trying to guess what a handful of insiders, huddled in secret meetings, have up their sleeves to steer the economy. It's wild—the market no longer directs interest rates; instead, a committee decides a desired direction for interest rates. It's crazy that a small group of often unelected individuals control the monetary policies that affect billions of lives.

For the sake of brevity, I am not going to go into the details of how the Bitcoin system works or the challenges that it has overcome. I am also simplifying many aspects of how it operates to illustrate certain key points. There are many outstanding resources on the technical and cryptographic challenges the Bitcoin protocols set out to grapple with, which created the Bitcoin network. I encourage you to dive deeper as your interest warrants. The wonderful thing is that, like a cell phone, you don't have to understand how it works to benefit from its usefulness.

BITCOIN'S FOUNDATION

The most significant aspect of Bitcoin is that its foundation is based on a clearly defined, rules-based system. It is established on first principles. Unlike our current monetary system, it is clearly and thoughtfully designed and engineered to include certain highly valuable properties, such as the permissionless, trustless, decentralized, and secure set of rules governing the system and its operation.

There is no Bitcoin board of governors. There are no elected or unelected leaders who decide how the system should operate. There is no president or CEO of Bitcoin. There are no majority shareholders. No corporation owns or runs it. Satoshi Nakamoto (whoever they are) hasn't been heard from since 2010.

No government created it, nor can any prohibit the operation of its worldwide network. There is no central database or computer that can be hacked or co-opted by authorities. Instead, there is only a set of rules and a network of people who decide for themselves whether the system and its rules are valuable to them, so they choose to participate.

Now, with no leader or someone "taking care" of users or telling them what to do or how to operate, personal responsibility and accountability are necessary. Individual sovereignty is a blessing, but it also comes with responsibilities. While a hardcore Bitcoiner might be focused solely on anonymous self-custody, such a model may not be as easy or desirable for others.

The protocol can suit the needs of a wide range of individuals, from those interested and experienced enough to be autonomous to those requiring custodial services. Corporations, organizations, and other entities can make different arrangements for security, stability, and longevity. All this is possible under the umbrella of the Bitcoin protocols, and as the system expands, more services and products will be developed to meet the needs of diverse users. Just as we have many ways to use and save money in our current monetary system (cash, checks, credit cards, electronic payments, bank accounts, brokerage accounts, trust services, and so on), different techniques for using and storing Bitcoin are, and increasingly will be, available to meet various requirements.

What is so fundamentally unique about Bitcoin is that no middleman is necessary—there are no gatekeepers or road-blocks—like when using a bank or financial institution. Right now, people in Africa who don't have access to banking but have a smartphone are using Bitcoin to save and transact. Bitcoin unleashes the ability to conduct financial transactions directly with anyone else around the globe for everyone on the planet. That is absolutely revolutionary!

All right, Tina. Sing us your song, "What's Love Got to Do with It." What do cryptography, software code, and network protocols have to do with love? That's a good question; I'm glad you asked.

RANDOM OR ORDERED?

The universe, the web of life, and all of creation can be viewed as either having underlying foundational principles or laws (protocols) or not. Either the universe is an all-encompassing phenomenon of randomness to which humans ascribe patterns—which, for convenience or comfort, they call rules but actually are not—or it is a system that works on fundamental underlying principles. In the same way, one can view consciousness as the interaction of chemicals in the brain (or somewhere) or as something more than that.

Materialist science and philosophy have pursued an approach to the universe wherein everything can be reduced to individual isolated constituents that happen to be interacting with each other. Admittedly, for much of my life, this was a view I shared. When I delved deeper and realized there was an alternative view that was both rational and intuitive, I cast off that old reductionist paradigm. This view is not based on blind faith but a deeper understanding birthed from learning about modern physics as well as Eastern and other wisdom traditions and my own experience and insight. It is also informed by the contemplation of the final unanswered question of the reductionist scientific view (to which it has no logical, verifiable, or intuitively satisfying answer): If everything is a random occurrence, where did it all start? What is the ultimate nature of reality?

If we wish to understand a watch, we can take it apart, examine all its components, see how they interact and operate, and then understand how it functions to keep track of time. But as we examine that watch, implicit in our knowledge of it is the understanding that there is a watchmaker. There is some intelligent organizing system implicit in the watch. Why isn't this also true of the universe? It makes no difference whether you want to call it a protocol, consciousness, natural law, or God. However, when it comes to religion, humans have gotten themselves into lots of trouble and conflicts by claiming to know who the watchmaker is and what he/she thinks and wants from us, including what the rules are and what the punishments are for not complying with those rules. The important point is that if there is a watch, there must also be principles that governed its creation, including a first principle and a protocol. Likewise, the universe has some organizing system or intelligence as its source and under which it operates, whether that be an omniscient, omnipresent entity or an evolutionary system of life and consciousness.

SOURCE CODE

It doesn't matter if you choose to call it God, nature, spirit, life, the prime mover, consciousness, beingness, or anything else. At the core of Eastern mystical traditions, many philosophical approaches, and most world religions is the concept of an all-encompassing consciousness connecting everything and from which all is sourced. Quantum physics, deep ecology, and the systems view of the web of life also reveal the interconnection and interdependence of the energetic forces and relationships between all things.

Life and consciousness exist in infinite forms. Some kind of protocol is guiding this energy and its interconnectedness. We could throw up our hands, not knowing what it is or what to call it, but why not call it love? Love is a familiar yet elusive concept. We can't cut open a heart to find it, smash rocks to uncover it, or logically define when it should or shouldn't happen. Love, like life and consciousness, remains a beautiful mystery.

What if we viewed "love" as the underlying protocol of life? Yes, I know love doesn't always show up in life the way we think it should look. But we also have to admit that our perspective is limited, and it's just going to be a fact of life that some paths people explore aren't paths of the heart. Yet we also know that "love makes the world go round." So, as Don Juan encouraged Carlos Castaneda, find the path with a heart. That path is good.

While Satoshi Nakamoto didn't explicitly declare Bitcoin as a symbol of love in the white paper, delve into Bitcoin's principles and protocols to explore the intent of its creation and educate yourself on its true essence. You may find, as I did, that Bitcoin can be a path with heart.

Money holds the power to store our labor's energy, allowing us to explore life's deeper meaning. Don't dismiss Bitcoin as mere magic Internet money for criminals without understanding it. What if we root money and the Bitcoin protocols in love? With love as the foundational principle, everything can shift. If we do this, it can pave the way for reimagining other systems, like finance, education, health, and relationships, to be truly based on love. It's worth considering.

Our opportunity, as well as our challenge, is to use "the protocol of love" to create the system we desire to live in, one that serves all of humanity while respecting the individual sovereignty of each living being. If we do, Bitcoin could be a new step on the path with heart and, therefore, good.

14

Permission to Love

Poor is the man whose pleasures depend on the permission of another.

— MADONNA CICCONE

CAN YOU IMAGINE A SYSTEM that required you to ask permission to love someone? We know that in some societies and cultures, parents arrange or grant consent for their children's marriages, but I'm talking about actual permission to love. We know that love does not depend on permission; it happens. It is not up to a central authority to dispense love.

Love itself is permissionless. It just is. It is present in

various forms and degrees without anyone needing to regulate it. Relationships of all forms are expressions of love. Intimate, familial, communal, and spiritual love are demonstrations of the innate and permissionless nature of love.

While trust makes loving relationships more easeful and harmonious, neither trust nor permission is required to love. We love our children even though they may not make trustworthy or sanctioned decisions. We love them, nonetheless. Our parents may have made considerable mistakes in raising us, but we can still love them.

THE NETWORK EFFECT

Love is a network of interactions of varying degrees of frequency, intensity, and strength. Each living being is a transmitter and a receiver. No human central authority is required. Life, God, the universe, or whatever you want to call it, is the field and the source of the energy of love. Your own experience verifies this, so you don't need some authority or science to prove it. It just is, even if it sometimes feels absent in your life.

At some time in your life, you have undoubtedly been with people or in circumstances where the network effect of love is palpable. A child looking into the eyes of its mother, lovers deeply connected in intimacy, the magnificence of a sunrise or sunset, the beauty of a flower, a mountain range's majesty, the endless expanse of the sea—what are these but love?

Humans have both physical outward senses and intuition to guide us through life. Our five senses process external data and phenomena. Our internal senses—gut feelings, intuition, foreboding, and feelings of love—guide us in other ways. All of our senses connect us to a vast network of life-forms, sentient or not, that is our universe. The fewer filters or limitations we place on sensing our experience of life, the richer and more powerful our experience will be.

SCIENCE CATCHES UP WITH EASTERN PHILOSOPHY

During recent history in the West, a philosophy of reductionism has dominated much of our worldview. Western philosophers and scientists dissect, distill, and separate matter and concepts in attempts to discern their essence. This practice reduces phenomena to machines operating as directed by physical, chemical, and electrical signals. While this approach has led to many important discoveries and benefits, it has also limited our perspective.

Modern quantum physics revealed that there are no ultimate reducible elements of matter (which atoms were once thought to be) from which all things are composed. That billiard ball analogy of atoms interacting with each other from high school physics does not capture reality as understood by modern quantum physics. Rather, everything is composed of energy and depends on the relative position of various energetic arrangements to other energetic arrangements, including the human observer.

Life sciences have evolved beyond a mechanistic view of discreet life-forms acting independently of each other and interacting only in limited chemical ways. Mother nature is a system. She is neither a discrete entity nor a controlling actor.

Fritjof Capra, in *The Systems View of Life: A Unifying Vision*, says, "Systems thinking is 'contextual,' which is the opposite of analytical thinking. Analysis means taking something apart in order to understand it; systems thinking means putting it into the context of a larger whole." Looking at a particular puzzle piece isn't that helpful. The trick is to put the pieces of the puzzle together!

The systems science described by Capra reveals a model of the universe that is inherently a network. Waves of energy emerge from the field, interact with each other, and fall back into the field. To those familiar with many Eastern spiritual traditions, you will see the same underlying structure described in those teachings, though they have been revealed through different forms of inquiry. Mystics, meditators, yogis, shamans, and the like have explored the nature of life for thousands of years and come to many of the same conclusions as modern scientists. We are part of an interconnected and interdependent network of life. This is the ultimate network effect.

We can also think of each of us as being part of a vast network of consciousness. Psychiatrist, teacher, and author of *Power vs. Force: The Hidden Determinants of Human Behavior*, Dr. David R. Hawkins, MD, PhD, put it this way:

> The individual human mind is like a computer terminal connected to a giant database. The database is human consciousness itself, of which our own cognizance is merely an individual expression, but with its roots in the common consciousness of all mankind. This database is the realm of genius; because to be human is to participate in the database, everyone, by virtue of his birth, has access to this genius.

As Chief Seattle of the Suquamish and Duwamish Native American tribes said, "Man does not weave this web of life. He is merely a strand of it. Whatever he does to the web, he does to himself."

Okay, Tina's asking, "What's Bitcoin got to do with it?"

CENTRALIZED LEDGERS

A function of money in our current monetary system is to serve as a ledger to account for who has (or owes) a certain amount of energy/money. When you deposit money at a bank, it records what you deposited in its ledger in addition to your withdrawals, borrowing and repayment of loans, and the interest paid to you on deposits. When you use a credit card for a transaction, a third party maintains a ledger of what you bought and what bank transfers must occur to settle the transaction between you and the business you bought something from.

These are all centralized ledgers. For this system to be functional and useful, the participants must trust the parties that maintain the ledgers. We must trust they will properly record and account for transactions, transfer funds as we direct, and safeguard the ledger. Centralized ledgers are useful and functional mechanisms for recording transactions and the movement of funds and have allowed the development of a huge network of financial relationships.

For money to move among parties, they must each have some relationship, either direct or indirect (for example, through a central bank), with each other. This is a centralized network. And, generally, every time one of those parties touches money, a little bit sticks to it and is lost in the process (bank fees, wire transfer fees, credit card fees, and so on). Centralized networks require permission to use them. If you don't meet certain requirements, you may be unable to use these systems. Much of the world's population is "unbanked" because they don't have access to the systems of centralized networks.

As discussed, a central authority introduces friction (fees) and inefficiencies into the system. Central authorities also pose an even bigger potential threat by allowing governmental entities to exert control over the ledger. Regardless of one's stance on the participants involved, governments have the power to manipulate accounts, freeze or confiscate funds, and regulate or forbid transactions. When individuals find they have lost access to their funds due to governmental restrictions carried out within a financial institution, trust in the system is eroded. While such control measures may be justified to prevent terrorism or criminal activities, people often have very different perspectives on these matters. Governments' use of centralized ledgers to control the finances of other nations, entities, or their citizens highlights the inherent risks associated with such systems.

Once we understand our financial system as a huge, interconnected network of thousands of central ledgers, we will see its vast complexity as well as its risks. If, for whatever reason, an error is made, a participant falls out of favor with the party that maintains the ledger, or the state requires money, a participant's wealth is subject to confiscation or taxation.

NODES

Bitcoin is a trustless, decentralized, and permissionless technology for the transfer of value between people. The Bitcoin network does not rely on a central authority to maintain a ledger. Nodes throughout the world maintain the Bitcoin network. Rather than a single party keeping or controlling the ledger, the nodes serve this function. Cointelegraph, a digital media website, describes a node this way:

> Nodes are the pillars of the Bitcoin network. These nodes continuously monitor the blockchain and its complete

transaction history to prevent access to non-legitimate trans-actions that attempt to spend their Bitcoin twice fraudulently, also known as the double-spending issue.

Any computer downloading the Bitcoin software that will join the Bitcoin network is called a node. The most popular client and software implementation of full nodes is Bitcoin Core; its latest release can be found on the GitHub page.

A node holds the complete history and chronology of the Bitcoin blockchain, which is like a ledger, and contributes to the security of the Bitcoin network through the consensus mechanism because nodes will reject any transaction that breaks consensus rules.

This new way of maintaining a ledger may take a little processing. Anyone can run a node on a computer, where the entire history of the transactions in the Bitcoin network can be downloaded and monitored. This is the essence of the decen-tralized network that is at the core of Bitcoin's ledger system. It provides transparency, consensus mechanisms, and security because there is no single point of failure.

While this ledger is often referred to as a blockchain, it is really a timechain of transactions. Each time a series of trans-actions (a block) occurs and is accepted by the nodes in the network, the transactions are time-stamped into the chain. This series of immutable transactions is one of the core features of the Bitcoin protocol. Every transaction that has ever and will ever occur on the main Bitcoin layer will be recorded, time-stamped, and fixed for all to see. No one can go back and change a trans-action because they cannot change the historical record in the timechain stored by all the nodes in the network. Can you see how this monetary network has the potential to look a lot more like our interconnected and interdependent web of life than a government-controlled one?

FREEDOM

We all have our own perspectives on life and love. The freedom to express them is an integral part of what it means to be a unique human being existing within the network of consciousness. Most of us value being able to interact with whomever we want and in any way we want. With a monetary system, however, people need to reach some consensus about an efficient and useful system.

The Bitcoin network allows each of us the potential to operate independently while offering a decentralized but consensus-building framework in which we can all participate. We can share our stored energy whenever and with whomever we want without needing a third party and without the friction (the fees) and the risk associated with having to channel our energy through a third party.

We don't want an authority in our homes telling us how we can share our love. Bitcoin is the first engineered network for the digital age that removes the need for a middleman and its attendant risks. Imagine a world where, with only the smartphone in your hand, you can transfer value to anyone else on the globe, 24/7/365 (yes, even on bank holidays!), without anyone or anything being in the middle, having to ask permission, or paying high fees to do so.

If we don't want to live in a system that requires permission to love someone, why would we want to live in a system that requires us to seek permission and trust a third party to transfer the energy of our labor if we don't have to?

15

Like Star-Crossed Lovers

*Any intelligent fool can make things bigger, more complex,
and more violent. It takes a touch of genius—and a lot of
courage—to move in the opposite direction.*

—E. F. SCHUMACHER

AS I'VE SHOWN, money is simply energy. The energy of our current or stored labor, whether physical, creative, or intellectual, is converted into the technology of money as a convenience mechanism. The "coincidence of wants" issue (barter isn't useful because I might not want what you have) is solved by the mechanism of money. Also, money makes accumulating and saving the excess energy associated with low time preference behaviors possible thanks to its function as a store-of-value technology.

Money is the map, not the territory. The technology that we use in our current system (fiat money—the map) to transfer or store value is inefficient, overly complex, corrupted, and violent. This map is without the integrity necessary to accurately represent the territory of the value created by human activity. Without the integrity necessary for sound money, fiat money and the actual energy of our labor are like star-crossed lovers because they are fated to a tragic outcome.

What we do in our lives to express our gifts, talents, industriousness, and interest in serving others is not strictly speaking impacted by or a function of the quality of our monetary system. However, when we convert those efforts into transferable currency units, the integrity of the system impacts how we transfer or store the value others assign to our efforts. And, when others siphon money off the system without providing concomitant value, the true value of our efforts is debased and devalued.

Back to the radio analogy. An individual's signal can be clear, pure, strong, and highly valued by others, but if it must be transmitted through a central party that distorts it, creates interference, and dilutes its strength, the power and integrity of their clear signal is affected. The use of money doesn't make the person's signal stronger, but it can weaken it.

In a system where a lot of effort goes into siphoning off the energy created by people under the guise of sophisticated financial products and machinations, we're draining our collective life force into activities that don't produce anything meaningful (though they might make some people rich). The credit and debt system, along with the constant devaluing of our currency, messes up how we allocate resources. We've shifted from working on farms and in factories to focusing on Wall Street, which we somehow call progress. Things like credit default swaps, foreign exchange hedging, and other complex financial products might generate revenue, but they are a symptom of a system where value is extracted instead of added; they contribute more to the problem than solving any real human need.

Most people feel good when they have done a good job at something. A craftsman making a beautiful and useful piece of furniture, a farmer growing nutritious food, or an artist creating music or a work of art that people intrinsically perceive as beautiful are all making both self-satisfying and societally useful contributions. The feedback mechanism for such work is that people are willing to trade the value of their efforts for those of others. Prices are assigned based on their perceived values in a market of many different participants.

When we go beyond a barter economy, the conversion technology is a system of money. Eventually, the money system begins to impact the variety and quality of the efforts expended. Instead of focusing on producing goods and services that contribute to actual societal value, effort becomes concentrated on what generates more of the society's units of money. Is that really worth devoting your life to? Money becomes a distorted signal. In fact, it can actually become the message when we operate in a society where people's primary interest is to accumulate more units of money. As Carlos Ruiz Zafón noted in his novel *The Shadow of the Wind*, "Making money isn't hard in itself...What's hard is to earn it doing something worth devoting one's life to."

Energy and the fiat money that is supposed to represent it become like star-crossed lovers; the two have a relationship, but it is destined to fail. There is a tragic flaw in a system where money/energy is not created by the love of the actors but by producers on the sidelines trying to extract money without any effort and talent by participants. The foibles of man being what they are, the power of the purse, coupled with the power to fill the purse without effort, have fated the relationship between the true energy of work and it's representation in fiat money to failure.

Many an empire has fallen due to its leaders overextending themselves and their people in a quest for power, dominion, and riches. When a nation's actions are limited to what the productivity of its citizenry can support, the monetary system maintains balance. Yet when they are unequally weighted, the scales of justice and society become unbalanced, such as when rulers pursue wealth through the spoils of war or the money printing often used to wage them.

The origin and operation of life and the universe are beyond the human mind's ability to comprehend. But we know that love acts as a connecting and harmonizing principle among a vast array of participants. Opposites can attract, and the like-minded can attract. Systems do not have to be fated to fulfill a controlling entity's will but can be functionally designed to accommodate all of the various participants. When the bonds are common, though the individuals' expressions of life may not be, we can avoid tragic outcomes.

16

Money, Wealth, Sex, and Love

Sex is like money; only too much is enough. — **JOHN UPDIKE**

AS WE DISCUSSED IN CHAPTER 6, high time preference behaviors emphasize short-term returns or pleasure over long-term investment or delayed gratification. Long-term investments become less attractive in a monetary system where it is challenging to convert and store the fruits of one's energy expenditure. We focus on superficial experiences now rather than choosing possibly deeper, longer-lasting, and more meaningful future experiences.

CULTURAL LEGACIES

As many in the Bitcoin community have pointed out, we see such preferences manifested in the arts, architecture, and music. To be an artist, someone once had to study for years to hone their ability to paint realistic and representational images. Today, someone can splatter paint on a canvas or slap it on in large blocks. Likewise, the magnificent architectural design and detail of the great buildings and monuments of culture, religion, history, and government have been replaced with concrete boxes that last less time than it used to take to erect buildings that still stand today. Our modern-built environment is now as disposable as a cardboard box.

These days, art like the *David* statue by Michelangelo and its testament to the magnificence of human form would no longer be revealed in marble but would be used as just another dude advertising some perfume. Great symphonies are replaced with indistinguishable electronic sounds generated by computer programs. Handcrafted goods are replaced with manufactured products. Don't get me wrong, there have been great achievements in manufacturing that have allowed people to live better lives, yet it seems like enduring and timeless creations of artistic expression have been sacrificed to convenience and consumption. If we are persuaded by advertising about what the "good life" looks like, we surrender our deepest values and desires to the gods of consumerism. Praying to this fleeting and transitory god is a false religion.

Historic centers of trade and commerce have been replaced with indistinguishable big-box stores. While some value Walmart for bringing its stores to underserved areas, I doubt many would suggest that a Walmart store rivals the Grand Bazaar in Istanbul, the ancient markets of Rome or Greece, the

Silk Road, or the historic shopping districts in most world cities.

When historians identify ancient civilizations as "great," they point to their arts, architecture, monuments, and religious buildings, many of which still exist today. The energy of the wealth of these societies endures both physically in these structures as well as in their contribution to the human condition. I'm not suggesting these societies were perfect, nor that their leaders were without avarice or a lust for power. Yet, there was also a quest for something grander—an enduring legacy—rather than the mundane. You don't build the Parthenon, the Taj Mahal, or a pyramid with a high time preference!

MEASURING "PRODUCTIVITY"

The wealth of a civilization is not measured by the number of things it produces. Gross domestic/national product (GDP or GNP) is a measure of activity (and an imprecise one), not of the outcomes of that activity. The fact that economies grow larger through more activity does not mean the well-being of their citizens is improving. Measuring productivity shows how we are so focused on producing and consuming more that we tend to give little thought to the quality of what we spend our time and energy on and whether it actually contributes to our happiness.

Bhutan has taken a revolutionary and novel approach by focusing on the nation's Gross National Happiness rather than traditional economic indicators. (Interestingly, Bhutan started Bitcoin mining several years ago and has reportedly mined over $1 billion dollars of Bitcoin from its hydropower resources.) The World Happiness Report was created to capture the idea that it is not simply economic production that is important, but it is the happiness of the nation's people. And, as it has shown, the countries with the highest GNP are not the ones highest in the happiness index rankings.

Arne Næss, the Norwegian philosopher who is credited with coining the term "deep ecology," said:

> GNP is therefore in a certain sense a value-neutral quantity: a measure of activity, not of activity of any kind of value. A first argument against continued growth is just this. The GNP does not give any guarantee of meaningfulness of that which is created. Growth in GNP does not imply any growth in access to intrinsic values and progress along the course of self-realization. Obviously any kind of economic growth which is not related to intrinsic values is neutral or detrimental. The measure of GNP is somehow related to the fierceness of activity in the society but this fierceness may very well have more to do with a lack of ability of the members of the society to engage in meaningful activity than a measure of something humanity should look upon with joy. There is no clear relation to life quality.

Producing more and more may create a larger economy, but is growth for growth's sake meaningful? Calculating how much stuff we create is a very dubious measuring stick for the true value of economic activity. Societies become driven to produce more goods faster and for less money regardless of the quality of those products or their contribution to quality of life. Disposable products contribute to a sense that life is also a disposable commodity. And many at the top of the business and governmental hierarchies treat people as disposable tools for their own self-aggrandizement.

QUALITY NOT QUANTITY

Isn't quality of life what we are all after? Don't we all seek love, happiness, and joy? When the energy of artists, creative geniuses, and lovers is reduced to high time preference activities, we end up not with great art, not with soaring architecture, and not with deep and timeless love stories.

So, let's dive deeper into relationships, love, and intimacy. The freedom born of cultural and societal changes has provided many people with opportunities to explore different paths in life. Even so, as it has always been in human history, the various systems we collectively operate within often influence the spheres of human behavior.

With a currency that rapidly devalues, holders are encouraged to transact today rather than save and invest in the future for themselves, their families, and their communities. While our individual lives may seem short, we are part of a timeless web of life. When we measure our actions only in terms of the money we have now and what we can spend it on to please ourselves without considering how we are contributing to life on this planet, we tend to consume without regard for future lives.

Seneca, in *On the Shortness of Life*, put it this way:

> It is not that we have a short time to live, but that we waste a lot of it. Life is long enough, and a sufficiently generous amount has been given to us for the highest achievements if it were all well invested. But when it is wasted in heedless luxury and spent on no good activity, we are forced at last by death's final constraint to realize that it has passed away before we knew it was passing. So it is: we are not given a short life but we make it short, and we are not ill-supplied but wasteful of it... Life is long if you know how to use it.

Our lives are not so much about living a short or long amount of time or about whether we live solely for today or also for the future. They are about finding balance and quality as we live them. Life is always lived and experienced in the now. It is not lived in the past nor in our regrets or errors. While individual lives are only experienced in the moment, life and consciousness transcend our limited experience of time. You can choose to experience and express love in your heart now as well as project it into the future for yourself and others.

RELATIONSHIPS

For many of us, there is a deep desire to share life physically, emotionally, and spiritually with an intimate partner. Just as water can be shallow and swiftly moving in a stream or deep and rolling in an ocean, relationships have different qualities. A hookup and a long-term relationship may both include sex, but one does not involve love, while the other (hopefully) does. Any mammal can rub genitals together, but true vulnerability and intimacy may be unique to humans.

High time preference behaviors in relationships are much like those in the economic world: someone caters to their desires now without depositing funds in the bank for long-term satisfaction. The tremendous growth of the porn industry capitalizes on a demand to satisfy desires immediately with just the browse of a website. Little investment is required, and little long-term satisfaction is achieved. Like a shopaholic who tries to fill their psychological and spiritual void with things yet is never satisfied, a porn addict also becomes compulsive and hooked on the fix from this stimulation. Though many find porn fun or convenient, we all know it's not love. It's a lot like when governments hand out money not backed by real energy and proof of work. It leaves us with a degraded and devalued experience.

Authentic, intimate relationships require time, effort, and commitment—in other words, a low time preference. Building lifelong relationships, just as in building lifetime wealth, requires quality in interactions, continual deposits of energy, and appreciation and respect for what is brought into the relationship. It's like doing an odd job for one day that feels relatively easy, but devoting ourselves to a lifetime career involves a lot more effort and energy. Love is easy, but loving relationships are not always so.

SEX

Among all the changes in attitudes concerning sex in the last decades, there has also been a movement to see intimate relationships from the view of ancient traditions, such as those in some Eastern philosophies, wherein intimate love was seen as a pathway to transcendence. Centuries of puritanical thought have denigrated the idea of intimate expression as a sacred path. But the journey of transcending the mundane is not a short one.

Like the difference between the characteristics of high and low time preference activities, truly making love generally requires a lower time preference orientation than most are accustomed to in sex. It's about slower sex and is based on sensitivity rather than just sensation. Rather than seeing sex as all about excitement and orgasm, we can see it as the slow exploration of our and our partners' bodies, where partners work with their deepest energies and offer this gift to each other.

Many teachings express that each person has inner masculine and feminine energies unconnected to gender or sexual orientation or expression. Some people have a stronger masculine essence, and some have a more feminine one. The salient point is that the masculine in all of us tends to be goal- and provider-oriented, action-driven, and outward-focused. The feminine tends to seek intimacy, safety (physical, emotional, sexual), and love. The interplay between these energies is what gives both power—and, often, confusion, disappointment, and conflict—in the sexual arena.

Sex depicted in the media, television, movies, novels, and certainly in the "adult entertainment" industry tends to be about using the other person for gratification and to achieve the goal of orgasm. It is usually demonstrated as wild passion, frantic friction, and brief bursts of energy.

On an episode of a TV show set in Paris, a young woman takes her boyfriend on a Ferris wheel famed for romantic encounters. She turns to him and says, "You have four minutes." Now, that might sound like a fantasy come true for a man with a high time preference, but I bet if you asked most feminine-essence women if such a scenario is appealing, the answer would probably be no.

It takes a low time preference orientation to engage in the slower sex of a deeper and more intimate relationship and to be willing to reeducate ourselves about habituated sexual behaviors. High time preference sex tends to be shallow and over quickly. Whether it is porn, a wham bam, thank you, ma'am hookup, or lovers who desire to connect but know little else, many take a pleasurable drink from a shallow pond when there is a deep ocean available to them.

Thich Nhat Hanh, a prominent and wise Vietnamese Buddhist teacher, speaks of "empty sex." He says:

Sexual desire is not love. Sexual activity without love is called empty sex. If you satisfy your body but don't satisfy your heart and your mind, are you satisfied? Do you feel whole and connected? When body, heart, and mind are satisfied, sexual intimacy connects you more deeply with yourself and your partner.

One of the deepest revelations of my life has been truly understanding and experiencing the difference between having sex and making love. The high time preference behavior and experience of the sex we see modeled in movies and novels is a short and shallow affair. Hot, frantic, explosive, and short-lived bursts of sexual energy are dramatic and can be pleasurable. But the feeling often lasts about as long as the proverbial cigarette afterward.

Just as I have suggested that we need to go beyond the technology of the currency of money to understand the true nature of money, we need to go beyond limited beliefs and practices that often comprise our approach to sex. Making love is tapping into and sharing the finer and more subtle energies that we as humans have access to. Sex for reproduction is one thing. Making love to transcend our individuality and touch the sacred is another.

The topic of sexuality is a long and winding road. My point is that society's approach to intimacy often mirrors its attitude in many other matters. Making money for money's sake is one thing, while channeling one's energy, talents, and creativity to express unique gifts to others is totally different. It depends if you want to stay in the shallow waters or dive deep. If you don't understand the difference between sex and love or between money and wealth, then, as Updike said, "Only too much is enough."

CHANGE

When we fully express our life force and feel the radiance of love within us, there is always enough. If we all truly operated from love, it would be a great place from which to build a freer, fairer, more compassionate and loving world.

Changing the monetary system is a long-term commitment. It won't instantly change behaviors, result in an explosion in the arts, or create lasting relationships and deeper intimacy. However, it is interesting to contemplate how societal systems interact and reinforce certain behaviors.

The systems and structures, whether economic, social, or spiritual, through which we live our lives reflect our values. If we aren't willing to demonstrate proof of work in our jobs, lives, and how we love, we diminish our gifts and capacity to love in favor of shallow ease and pleasure. Moreover, if we value centralized or authoritarian control, consumption now versus investing for the future of our children and planet, and acquiescence to transactional relationships and the aggrandizement of the politically powerful, our systems will reflect that.

On the other hand, if we value the sovereignty of all individuals, honor and respect our differences and contributions, and desire healthy and harmonious communities and environments, we can design and engineer systems that are conducive to these values. The thing is, if a society's values are questionable, no monetary system is going to "fix" them.

I'll repeat the quote I mentioned earlier because it is critical to understand the way lasting change occurs. R. Buckminster Fuller famously and quite rightly suggested, "You never change things by fighting the existing reality. To change something, build a new model that makes the existing model obsolete." If we desire to change our existing models, then we must build a new model and new systems that will attract energy to them.

If we conceive of love as the underlying field from which consciousness, life, matter, and all things arise, then let that be the measure by which we can examine our existing reality, its structures, and any potential new ones. Are they in alignment with love or not? And if a new model based on love exists, the old paradigm will dissolve when the new model attracts enough energy. And while this can happen nonviolently and without struggle, dislocations and unease are part of any change. Those who are entrenched in and are the primary beneficiaries of existing systems will naturally not embrace change, which may result in conflict. If the operators of the old paradigms and models resist, violent conflict could result. But if we shift our perspective and paradigm to the protocol of love, we can create a freer, fairer, more peaceful, and more loving world with constructive, rather than destructive, change.

The proponents and voices of the new system will need to demonstrate by word and action that the new model is a better model for everyone, not just them. When I look around at the true, deeply educated, and committed members of the Bitcoin community, I hear a myriad of these voices. The cacophony of the ignorant and entrenched powers is loud. We can shout epithets at each other, but the world is so filled with polarized arguments that the message often dies in a din of noise. Instead, let ours be the embracing message of love.

17

Scarcity, Abundance, and Division

The greatest scarcity in the world is not the scarcity of resources. It's the scarcity of imagination and vision.

—ANIL KUMAR GAIN

WHEN WE DIVIDE OURSELVES BY LABELS—progressive, libertarian, left-wing, right-wing, conservative, liberal, religious, or non-believer—we do ourselves a disservice. "Divide and conquer" means that by inciting division in people it is far easier to conquer them. The more we allow people to divide us with labels, the easier we will be conquered. With eight billion people on the planet, we will have diverse views and perspectives.

PLURALITY WITHIN SINGULARITY

Most don't wish for only one kind of flower in their gardens; instead, they relish the beauty of diverse colors, textures, fragrances, shapes, and sizes. This is also how people's differing values and perspectives should be viewed. The most dangerous human is the one who is absolutely convinced of the correctness and righteousness of their beliefs and feels compelled to foist them on others.

There is a difference between explaining a perspective or arguing a point in a respectful dialogue and proselytizing. Very little is gained through polarization and demonization. The demons are our shadows. If we don't do our work and understand our shadows, we tend not to grow and evolve past the shadows we all have.

The ocean could be divided into individual droplets, each with its own point in time and space, but any one of them alone would be meaningless. Yet without all these myriads of droplets, there would be no ocean. Life and creation are the never-ending flow of droplets within the vast ocean of the universe. The individuality of life and matter is but an expression of the totality.

The human mind constructs all sorts of labels for and divisions among humans. While the expression of energy may be different in each form, they share the same underlying energy. We can value both. We get into trouble, however, when we focus on division rather than commonality. Jiddu Krishnamurti put it like this: "When you call yourself an Indian or a Muslim or a Christian or a European, or anything else, you are being violent. Do you see why it is violent? Because you are separating yourself from the rest of mankind."

The amazing thing about *Life, the Universe and Everything*

(to quote the title of Douglas Adams's book) is that plurality exists within singularity. Each must be acknowledged, respected, and fully participated in. To lack this understanding is a symptom of ignorance, as are the divisions, such as hatred, anger, and exploitation we find among people. If we shift our perspective to seeing "evil" as ignorance and a lack of awareness, it is far easier to have compassion. From this place, we can engage in respectful dialogue and the sharing of ideas and perspectives. Perhaps we just might learn we don't know everything after all!

ABUNDANCE

One of the most famous Eastern wisdom texts, the *Isha Upanishad*, is the subject of the book *Liberation* by Anand Mehrotra. It begins with this beautiful expression:

> This is full and that is full, and
> This full has come out of that full.
> And even though this full
> has come out of that full, that
> full maintains its fullness.

The source (whatever that may be) of all the energy in the universe is characterized by limitlessness and abundance. Though all form—this full—came from that full, that full is still full. Money comes from that full, but that full is still full. The fullness behind the universe is not limited; it is not scarce. Nor is there duality between this and that, me and you, or human consciousnesses and the universe. Astronomer Carl Sagan noted, "The cosmos is within us. We are made of star stuff. We are a way for the universe to know itself."

The universe is infinitely abundant in energy. Consider that the amount of the sun's energy is beyond most humans' ability to conceive, yet it is a small star within a small solar system in a small galaxy in a universe extending beyond our capacity of comprehension. What is limited is our ability to harness and use the energy of the universe, given our current understanding and technologies. What is scarce is not the energy of the universe but the willingness and effort of much of humanity to transcend the mundane to the deeper spheres of understanding and wisdom.

Usable energy is different from the totality of energy. Harnessing usable energy requires work, whether drilling for oil, building wind turbines, mining coal, or building photovoltaic cells to capture the sun's energy; channeling this energy requires demonstrable effort. Thus, the abundance of the universe is channeled through what is scarce—the real work of humans.

As we've discussed, money is simply a means of tracking this scarce work. Logic and reality refute the concept that unlimited money can be created from what is scarce—the human time and effort required to do work. Yet this is what governments and central bankers have convinced us they can do. While the Norse god Thor may have been able to harness the energy of thunder, that's a task better left to the gods than to central bankers!

THE POWER OF SCARCITY

Scarcity is a valuable concept when attempting to capture and not dilute the value of the energy we seek to convert to the technology of money through our work. The energy's source, however, is not scarce. But neither is that energy a matter of proof of stake.

Many cryptocurrencies, other than Bitcoin, rely on a "proof of stake" concept. Coins are created by the developers who maintain a large stake before selling them to others. Then, those with the largest stakes get to make the rules. But just because someone has a bigger stake does not mean they are a larger source of true value creation. As I discussed earlier, Bitcoin is unique in that it operates on a "proof of work" framework. Work—energy—must be expended to create new Bitcoin in accordance with the protocols. It doesn't matter who does it; what does matter is that real energy is required. This gives the system integrity.

The solar energy that makes all life possible on earth is not limited to what humans, animals, or plants can capture from the sun's rays on this little blue dot. Some of that energy is captured and converted through humanity's efforts. Mining metals, fabricating steel to build buildings, practicing the healing arts, farming food, creating art or music, or probing and distilling eternal and timeless concepts to share with others are all "proof of work." When others see any of this as valuable, they share some of the value of their energy, created through their proof of work, in exchange for it.

The value of scarcity is a crucial underpinning of the Bitcoin protocol because it prevents Bitcoin's devaluation by the continuous expansion of its supply. The protocol defines the rules for generating Bitcoin and imposes a cap of twenty-one million on the total number of Bitcoins that can ever exist. The system's difficulty adjustment governs the rate at which a block of transactions is added to the blockchain and new Bitcoin is brought into circulation.

Approximately every four years, the reward for successfully "mining" Bitcoin is halved. Approximately 99 percent of all the Bitcoin that can be created will be released in the next ten years. Over the next hundred years, the final few Bitcoins will slowly be created, ending around the year 2140. This unique feature ensures that, unlike the fiat currency system, where more units can be continuously created, the number of new Bitcoins diminishes over time. After the last Bitcoins are created, transaction fees, as well as the value received by all of the participants, will be the ongoing incentive to maintain the system.

This scarcity principle reflects a meticulously crafted monetary policy that remains unaltered by economic conditions, political influences, or the decisions of elected or unelected officials. The Bitcoin protocol's predetermined scarcity is a deliberate feature designed to provide a level of predictability and resistance to external manipulation.

With no dilution or the destruction of value from debasement and inflation, each Bitcoin and its subunits (referred to as satoshis or sats) accrue value corresponding to the increasing energy stored in the system. The energy is not scarce, nor is the storage capacity. Each Bitcoin is divisible into sats, each representing one one-hundred-millionth of a Bitcoin (one hundred million sats equal one Bitcoin). There is infinite capacity to store energy in Bitcoin as well as account for and transfer small amounts within the system. The value of humanity's work to be stored in Bitcoin as a monetary system is not created by Bitcoin mining—it is simply the reward for doing work (computational) that secures the network and the timechain of transactions. The value of Bitcoin is in the energy it stores.

The price of Bitcoin in dollars (or other currencies) rises as the value of the energy stored in the system increases. Compare this to how currency units in fiat systems are being debased. As people transfer from other currencies or assets to Bitcoin, the amount of energy in the system increases compared to the energy in other systems. The increasing value of Bitcoin (as denominated in fiat currencies) is not some gamble paying off for holders. The ultimate cause is that more people are storing more energy in the system and using that system to transfer greater amounts of value. It is a very different concept from stocks, bonds, or real estate, where the asset's value is determined by supply and demand, expected growth rates, or the discounted value of cash flows. It is a fundamentally different asset, so the models from other traditional assets don't apply. This is why so many fail to grasp the framework for understanding how to assess the price of Bitcoin; they are thinking in fiat terms.

Let's use an example of a simple economy to highlight the impact of a defined monetary policy with a scarce number of units of money like Bitcoin. If people in a community do one hundred hours of equally valued work and there are one hundred units of money in the system, each hour of work would be worth one unit. When another hundred hours of work is performed and saved in the existing hundred units of currency, each unit now holds the value of two hundred hours of work. Let's call the currency units dollars. So, each dollar has now gone from representing one hour of work to two hours of work. As a result, the energy in the dollar has gone up, so the value of the currency rises compared to the price of goods. Value added to a limited supply of currency makes prices go down, not up!

DILUTION IS NOT THE SOLUTION

Contrast this with our current system, where central banks continually add more units so the energy/value of each unit declines and prices rise. Let's make this a bit more realistic by adding consumption into the system. If a community does one hundred hours of work equal to one hundred units of money, much of that will be consumed for food, fuel, and other nondurable goods. If people were able to save 5 percent of what they produced instead of consuming it, they could begin the process of building wealth unless someone continually dilutes the value of what they earn and save.

If the government adds new units of money to the system every year at a rate of 7 percent, then what happens is that, instead of growing wealth by saving 5 percent of one's work a year, the system is diminishing the value of the currency and the work. Even if they can save, people get poorer every year by 2 percent. Many people struggle to save anything, and most of the money they earn from their labor goes into current consumption. Thus, if wages don't rise by 7 percent a year to keep pace with the rate that dollars are increased in the system, people fall behind rather than get ahead as the value of their labor in dollars keeps falling because new dollars (without any actual contribution of work) are continually being introduced into the system.

While the consumer price index (CPI), the official measure of inflation, gets all the attention, little is paid to the monetary inflation rate. As I discussed previously, CPI is an artificial and inaccurate measure of the true increase in the cost of goods. The other factor that doesn't make as many headlines is the amount of new money continually being added to the system.

Historically, in the United States, the rate of increase in the monetary supply (called M2) has been about 7 percent per year. This means that unless your wages and the value of your savings are increasing at a rate equal to or greater than 7 percent, you are falling behind and not getting ahead. And this is the "best money" in the world! In many other countries, the rate of monetary growth, often referred to as "money printing," is far, far higher. This leads to the devastating impacts of declining currency values and hyperinflation. Productivity increases and technological improvements that add real value diminish some of the effects, but this is little comfort when these improvements should lead to falling, rather than rising, prices.

Because the money supply isn't something people normally think about, it might take some digesting to understand it. Central banks are like the Wizard of Oz, who tells us to pay no attention to the man behind the curtain, as they create more and more money without any true value being added. Hopefully, the impact of Bitcoin's monetary policy with its scarce, rather than increasing, number of units is becoming clearer. A limited number of units accrue the value of more and more energy over time, and so their value rises infinitely compared to the price of goods as the value of new work is stored in them. This is why the statement that "Bitcoin is going up forever" isn't as crazy as it first sounds. That, though, is from a fiat perspective, where we price Bitcoin in a fiat currency. What is more significant is that with more value stored in Bitcoin, the prices of goods continually fall, especially since technology and productivity improvements are making the cost of producing goods cheaper.

Some have rather laughably posited that an economy is restricted and will implode without an expanding money supply. This is confusing the source of the energy with the units of storage. A hundred thousand Argentine pesos is a lot of units of currency, but it is exchanged for a lot fewer units in US dollars (less than $150 at the time of this writing). It's not the units; it's the energy—which is not generated by the number of units or paper! If more units were actually valuable, then Venezuela wouldn't have to keep chopping zeros off its currency as it has done multiple times. This should make the silliness of this game and the reality of the actual problem clear. In Venezuela, one day, you need a million-bolivar bill to buy a loaf of bread, and the next day, the government chops off six zeros, so then it costs one bolivar. And a few years later, they do it again. Real work and real value aren't what are expanding—things are not getting cheaper—the currency is just being diluted by the hyper-inflationary impacts of poor monetary and economic policies.

NO LONGER RISK-FREE

Many economists, academics, politicians, financiers, and invest-ment professionals don't really understand what money is. All they know is they want more of the units themselves. I spent two decades in investment management and was a Certified Financial Planner ®, and no one I encountered in the financial world ever taught, based advice, or formulated coherent strate-gies and plans with a clear understanding of what money really is. It isn't taught; it isn't understood.

As I shared in chapter 2, government-created inflation propels the need to "invest" because we can't just save our money and preserve its purchasing power. The trouble is that even traditional investment theories and approaches no longer make much sense. The main idea behind investment allocation is called "modern portfolio theory," though it was introduced in 1952, so it's not exactly modern. The theory is about risk diversification and recommends comparing different investment options to the "risk-free" rate of return on US Treasury bonds. The goal is to figure out the best mix of investments for the most reward, given their risk levels.

However, there are issues with the theory. It was developed when the US was the ascendant global power and was still on the gold standard, so the idea of a "risk-free rate" made more sense back then. When you add the excessive levels of both public and private debt, tremendous leverage, and the increasing size of financial crises in the US economy, which result in ever more money printing, US Treasuries look a lot less "risk-free" now.

Recently, when the United States Federal Reserve quickly increased interest rates, it caused major declines in bond values and big losses in US Treasuries that led to some major banks failing. The volatility of and negative return on US Treasuries means that they are now anything but "risk-free." The United States is so deeply in debt that if it were an individual or a corporation, it would have been declared bankrupt long ago. The same is true of many countries around the world. The only way out is to either raise taxes and cut spending to repay the debt or to keep printing money. The former is unlikely, so the latter is nearly guaranteed to continue.

Given that US Treasuries have been severed from any real economic foundation and the explosion of government-created money, the concept of US Treasuries being risk-free is laughable. Oh, I'm not saying investors won't be paid back—it's just that the actual value of the purchasing power they receive will be significantly diminished. This represents the real risk and real harm that is a by-product of dilution. It is a reality that if fully understood could foment great societal discord and division. At the very least, it will compel greater governmental spending constraints or it may result in a collapse of the entire debt-based system, requiring a huge financial reset if not an entirely new monetary system.

ACCOUNTING FOR THE REAL COSTS

If we sink into a mindset that only our current individual needs matter and resources are fundamentally scarce, a "grab-all-we-can-get-while-we-can" attitude takes hold. In this framework, extracting as much energy as possible from the system while contributing little in return is rational behavior. With such a limited perspective, it seems to work. Though we see many who add great value—and may or may not accrue great stores of energy/money for it—we also see those whose contributions are negligible or extractive yet accrue vast resources for that as well. Self-aggrandizingly siphoning off the energy contributed by others results in disharmony in the system.

Governments often want to spend resources for either well-intended purposes or for more questionable causes like "pork-barrel" projects. The sums of money politicians want to spend are often beyond the people's productive capacity and willingness to be taxed. When governments resort to creating more units of currency, the value of the energy stored by the people in those units is debased. This inflation acts as an insidious stealth tax on those who can least afford it.

The transmission lines are leaking energy at an accelerating pace, so more money must be pumped through the system to keep things running. Just like the electrical grid, eventually, breakdowns happen, blackouts occur, and darkness spreads. Ultimately, balance will be restored in the system, but the longer our out-of-control debt-based system continues, and the more extreme the situation becomes, the more painful the reset will be.

We lack the ability, technology, or perhaps even the conceptual framework to calculate the full cost of our actions. If we could consider all their consequences and factor them into our decisions, it would be easier to see the true costs. Imagine a company dumping toxic waste into a river—it might seem less expensive than disposal costs, but if we accounted for the harm caused to people through their drinking water, the true price to society would be considerable. Currently, profit drives companies to use the easiest and cheapest waste disposal method, which leads to lower costs and enables lower prices for the product and/or higher profits for those benefiting. If we could link the costs of pollution (health as well as cleanup) back to the company, it would then be reflected in the price of the product. Any advantage from dumping waste would likely disappear, eliminating the benefit of harmful actions.

Similarly, if we could attribute the economic harm caused by printing too much money back to politicians and bureaucrats, they would authorize spending with more constraint and accountability. Yet, the power of the purse (held by both legislators and lobbyists) can buy a lot of votes to maintain power and influence. They figure their purses will be full long before anyone turns ours inside out to find them empty!

When we ditch the distorted evolutionary idea that only the strongest survive, things look different. With a broader awareness, embracing the idea that "whatever you do to the least of my brothers, you do to me" (as Jesus said), we start valuing unity and connection over separation. It's like seeing both sides of a coin—one is individuality, the other is unity. Bringing these opposite sides together brings harmony and the understanding that there's plurality within unity and unity within plurality.

18

Technology, Sovereignty, and the Loving Resistance Fighter

Technology gives us power, but it does not and cannot tell us how to use that power. Thanks to technology, we can instantly communicate across the world, but it still doesn't help us know what to say. —**RABBI LORD JONATHAN SACKS**

THE EXPLOSION IN THE DEVELOPMENT AND USE of new technologies has revolutionized how we interact and how we are interacted with. From email to social media and from Amazon to mobile banking, the scope and convenience of technological connections and transactions have morphed from a physical, analog age to a digital age where communication and information are global, near-instant, and widely accessible. While this has provided significant benefits, it also comes with costs.

The abuse of technology platforms to monitor behavior, track our activities, and censor speech is becoming more rampant. Even more profoundly concerning is that we are moving from an age where technology was a tool to serve humankind's aspirations to an age where technology is becoming the predominant force. As technology becomes the driver of human activity and the arbiter of truth, traditional cultural values, historical narratives, and millennia of wisdom traditions get pushed aside as we become reduced to economic units that serve the interests of the corporate nation-state.

THE INFORMATION AGE

Where once access to information was restricted and limited to academics, elites, governments, intermediaries, and the keepers of the flames of knowledge, the fire is now available to illuminate all. There is a difference, however, between information, knowledge, and wisdom, which I will discuss further below.

Most systems to facilitate access to information and communication were developed by centralized sources. When Google set out on the noble goal to digitize every book ever printed, it heralded a new era, both in what was accessible and how it was accessible. Intermediaries like Google and Facebook offered services and information many of us found very useful; thus, due to the network effect, they expanded rapidly to encompass billions of people worldwide since the access they offered seemed like it was free. Then, their market shares exploded, enabling them to become monopolistic entities. Nouns become verbs when everyone just "googles" the information.

What is less transparent is what we gave up in exchange

for information access. The business and social culture in the "developed West" is dominated by advertising and marketing. We are constantly bombarded with messaging to influence our likes, desires, behaviors, and purchasing decisions. In the broadcast television age, it seemed an acceptable trade-off for the entertainment it funded. We could walk away during what were obvious commercials, and what we viewed was not directly traceable or trackable back to us. We did not knowingly or unknowingly surrender personal information about our interests, tastes, and habits when we turned on the TV.

In the digital age, nearly every action we take online is tracked, fed into algorithms, and spit back at us to attempt to capture our attention and money. By now, we all know elements of how insidious and devious this system is. From inciting angst and hatred through the powerful fuels of fearmongering and divisive and enraging content to the manipulation of the "truth" for political, governmental, or economic motives, the systems' and advertisers' needs are prioritized, and not the users'. We are pawns in a chess game, and most of humanity has little understanding or awareness of how they are being played.

Users have surrendered their life information to centralized online intermediaries who monetize this information for the benefit of others. Yet, obviously, if the tech users didn't receive value from them, they wouldn't use the platforms. While we all implicitly understand that nothing is free, what we are giving up is both subtle and opaque.

Regulators are trying to bring some level of transparency and protection to what happens to user data, but the business model is so lucrative that data abuses are rampant and routine. Facebook, for example, was the subject of a US Federal Trade Commission (FTC) order in 2012 over data use, but violated that order and, in 2019, paid a record $5 billion fine for "deceiving users about their ability to control the privacy of their personal information."

It is one thing to be browsing online for shoes and have shoe advertisements pop up; it's another to have our news feed constructed based on the algorithm's analysis of our political interests or leanings. That free Gmail account comes at the cost of allowing Alphabet Inc. to scan all our emails to distill information from them and direct messages to us based on what it finds. Suppose whenever we sent a letter through the mail, we knew that the postal service would read every word and use it to support the government's objectives and control over us. I doubt very many people would drop a letter in the box. Prisoners in jail understand that the warden is entitled to open all incoming and outgoing correspondence. That is the price paid for committing a crime. Is it a price worth paying when no crime has been committed?

CENTRALIZATION VERSUS AUTONOMY

So, where will we draw the lines on the trade-offs between access to these technological tools and surrendering our information and privacy to centralized intermediaries? Are there viable alternatives? And what principles do we wish to operate under both individually and as part of a community? These are the questions we need to ask rather than unthinkingly resigning ourselves to the existing systems.

Government monitoring of Internet use is another layer of grave concern. Freedom House issued a report written by Adrian Shahbaz in 2018 titled "The Rise of Digital Authoritarianism," which included the following:

The Internet is growing less free around the world, and democracy itself is withering under its influence.

Disinformation and propaganda disseminated online have poisoned the public sphere. The unbridled collection of personal data has broken down traditional notions of privacy. And a cohort of countries is moving toward digital authoritarianism by embracing the Chinese model of extensive censorship and automated surveillance systems...

With or without malign intent, the Internet and social media in particular can push citizens into polarized echo chambers and pull at the social fabric of a country, fueling hostility between different communities...

Securing Internet freedom against the rise of digital authoritarianism is fundamental to protecting democracy as a whole. Technology should empower citizens to make their own social, economic, and political choices without coercion or hidden manipulation. The Internet has become the modern public sphere, and social media and search engines have both tremendous power and a weighty responsibility to ensure that their platforms serve the public good. If antidemocratic entities effectively capture the Internet, citizens will be denied a forum to articulate shared values, debate policy questions, and peacefully settle intrasocietal disputes. Democracy also requires a protected private sphere. The unrestrained and largely unexamined collection of personal data inhibits one's right to be let alone, without which peace, prosperity, and individual freedom—the fruits of democratic governance—cannot be sustained or enjoyed.

If democracy is to survive the digital age, technology companies, governments, and civil society must work together to find real solutions to the problems of social media manipulation and abusive data collection. Multilateral and cross-sectoral coordination is required to promote digital literacy, identify malicious actors, and deny them the tools to fraudulently amplify their voices. When it comes to protecting data, users must be granted the power to ward off undue intrusions into their personal lives by both the government and corporations. Global internet freedom can and should be the antidote to digital authoritarianism. The health of the world's democracies depends on it.

The access to and use of our personal information and the infringement on our privacy are issues that warrant collective concern. Establishing boundaries on government access and use of our data must involve a delicate balance between safeguarding user privacy and facilitating lawful investigations into potential criminal activities. All of us must recognize the significant threats that could result if we don't grapple with these challenges. Awareness is key in navigating the complexities of personal privacy and security and the legal considerations regarding them in the digital age. Powerful interests in big tech and government have little incentive to truly protect our privacy. Questionable but politically appealing justifications ("fighting terrorism") are consistently used to whittle away at the privacy of our communications.

While there is a natural inclination to create government rules and regulations in an attempt to control the use and abuse of these platforms, we must be cautious about this knee-jerk reaction. Given the close ties (and flow of campaign contributions) between many technology companies and the politicians that could regulate them, we could end up with backdoor state-sanctioned monopolies that have even deeper control. As Robert Heinlein, in his novel *Red Planet* has his wise old character Doc say, "Every law that was ever written opened up a new way to graft."

For Internet and social media platforms, we need to consider if other models might strike a better balance. While the current framework was built on the century-old advertising-revenue model, other models are possible and perhaps preferable. If the choice is to pay a small monthly subscriber fee to own and be in control of your information, might that be worth it?

Or, what if we stand the current paradigm on its head? Instead of surrendering our personal information for its monetization by intermediaries and advertisers, what if we could monetize access to our own information ourselves? What about a system where we could control and monetize our interests and purchasing habits rather than the other way around? Technology systems, networks, and cost structures are so advanced that centralized intermediaries are not absolutely required.

Transitioning from centralized systems to decentralized systems, whether in social networks or monetary systems, will be a paradigm shift. The more we understand the risks of centralized systems and the benefits of decentralized ones, the more the desire for such transitions gains momentum.

For example, the social media platform X (formerly Twitter) owns and controls all the information on the platform. The "Twitter files" released in 2022–2023 revealed that the US government worked closely with Twitter to remove accounts and suppress certain information being disseminated on the site. If you tweeted something that was deemed "misinformation," you risked being booted from the system.

New platforms such as Nostr have arisen to allow account holders to own the information they post and to shape their interactions with others. Nostr allows for "Zaps" where users can transfer value in the form of sats (the Bitcoin subunits we discussed earlier) and thereby reward information viewed as valuable. Rather than users providing content for free to the platforms that use it to make money for themselves, the content providers own and monetize the information themselves. Instead of a centralized platform on which all information is owned and controlled by a single entity like X, Nostr is a decentralized platform. This is a developing and revolutionary paradigm shift in social media and information platforms.

Secure email systems that offer end-to-end encryption and prioritize users' rights over corporate interests are now more widely available. With relatively little effort, we can begin the shift to protecting our privacy and rights rather than allowing them to be surreptitiously compromised. It's time to think about giving up our free Gmail accounts, as they make us the product rather than the consumer. We should opt for more secure systems that prioritize the security of user information and data rather than using it for the goals of big tech.

FROM TOOLS TO TECHNOPOLY

While it is critically important to understand sovereignty, the creeping intrusion on personal privacy, and the abuse of control mechanisms made possible by modern technology, it is even more crucial to understand the role technology has in influencing and shaping cultural and societal norms. Neil Postman, in his book *Technopoly: The Surrender of Culture to Technology*, frames the issue by defining three technological ages. The first, which dominated most of human history, is the tool-using stage. Humans (the *homo faber* in Arendt's system we discussed in chapter 6) developed various tools (the bow and arrow, wheel, etc.) that improved our ability to perform specific tasks. However, the development of these tools did not challenge or disrupt the dominant cultures or belief systems. Instead, these tools served humans within these structures.

In the second age, which he calls "Technocracy," tools begin to play a central role in society, and the developing technologies start to challenge traditional culture, belief systems, and institutions. The development of the telescope, revealing that the earth is not the center of the universe but rather revolves around the sun, severely challenged and threatened the then-dominant beliefs and institutional structures. In this age, tensions developed between the old values and the discoveries and powers unleashed by new technologies.

In the final age, which he refers to as "Technopoly," technology becomes the dominant force and central authority in society. In this stage, cultural history, beliefs, and practices become subsumed by society's focus on information, efficiency, and the rapidly evolving benefits and demands of new technologies. Technology is no longer a supportive tool but the primary driving force in society, defining and controlling its culture.

A simple and perhaps benign example is something we've all experienced. When asking a question or requesting information, the only answer, no matter its accuracy, is, "Well, the computer says...," and that becomes the truth. More deviously, technology has become the primary cause of information overload, the plethora of new data (often relatively meaningless) "proving" something, and the growing deference to computer outputs. Scientific studies backed by reams of data made available by technology can be used to "prove" nearly anything.

As Postman describes, science has been invaluable as we try to understand the natural process of the universe. "Science," however, when applied to the practices of human behavior, is a far more questionable undertaking. As the never-ending stream of data made possible by technology is used in the social sciences to define the "truth" of human behavior, we lose the perspectives formed by thousands of years of cultural traditions, mores, and standards. This technology-backed science begins to be the arbiter of what humans "should" do rather than humanity being guided by the perspective, judgment, and wisdom accumulated over the thousands of years of its history.

Postman wrote his book over thirty years ago, long before the dominance of now-ordinary devices and the further expansion of technology's influence on everyday life. If we reflect on the impact of technology in these last few decades (even before the nascent advent of AI), it is obvious that technology has dramatically affected our lives. What is less obvious but worthy of contemplation is how it has affected our cultural institutions, values, individual responsibilities, and social beliefs.

Postman frames it this way:

> Technopoly is a state of culture. It is also a state of mind. It consists in the deification of technology, which means that the culture seeks its authorization in technology, finds its satisfactions in technology, and takes its orders from technology. This requires the development of a new kind of social order and of necessity leads to the rapid dissolution of much that is associated with traditional beliefs. Those who feel most comfortable in Technopoly are those who are convinced that technical progress is humanity's supreme achievement and the instrument by which our most profound dilemmas may be solved. They also believe that information is an unmixed blessing, which through its continued and uncontrolled production

and dissemination offers increased freedom, creativity, and peace of mind. The fact that information does none of these things—but quite the opposite—seems to change few opinions, for such unwavering beliefs are an inevitable product of the structure of Technopoly. In particular, Technopoly flourishes when the defenses against information break down.

As I have argued in this book, there is a price to be paid when we wander far from deeper universal principles and from inquiry into our values and responsibilities, both as individuals and as part of a greater interconnected universe. We must foster but also harness the great technological developments of our current and coming ages to serve a more meaningful quest than the one for more data, greater efficiency, or more money.

Postman summarizes,

> The Technopoly story is without a moral center. It puts in its place efficiency, interest, and economic advancement. It promises heaven on earth through the convenience of technological progress. It casts aside all traditional narratives and symbols that suggest stability and orderliness, and tells, instead, of a life of skills, technical expertise, and the ecstasy of consumption. Its purpose is to produce functionaries for an ongoing Technopoly.

I am not a Luddite. We can embrace new technologies while directing them to serve deeper purposes. We must not become victims to those whose lust for power and control is enhanced through the tools of technology that would turn us into "functionaries" for an ever-growing governmental and corporate Technopoly.

So, what do we do? Postman advises, "You must try to be

a loving resistance fighter." I think that is a noble and worthy role and one quite applicable to proponents of Bitcoin. But each element of that is critically important. The first is to be loving. That is, after all, the central theme of this book. The second is to resist the creeping intrusions of the corporate nation-state on our individual liberties and to resist power structures that exert control and extract rather than add value. And lastly, be a fighter. I suggest we view this in the light of being a spiritual warrior. It is not about taking up arms to fight but about being strong in our convictions, acting with balance and integrity, and following a path guided by deep wisdom rather than the shallow desperation for money, power, or control.

So, speaking of those things, let's turn to a hot topic requiring us to be Postman's loving resistance fighters.

CENTRAL BANK DIGITAL CURRENCIES

Our current money system is a bit like Google or Facebook—it's centralized, and if you want to use it, you must follow the authority-in-charge's rules and give up whatever info they ask for. In the United States and elsewhere, our financial system used to be based on private, untraceable cash transactions. But now, it's mostly about transactions through systems that intermediaries and governments can access, trace, and often control. The US government, along with others, demands a lot of reporting within this financial system. Big transactions, moving money across borders, and holding assets outside the United States all must be reported to the government. As a result, once they know what you have and where it is, it is a simple matter to slap restrictions on using it.

As Lyn Alden in *Broken Money* discusses, while there is a general agreement of support for fighting criminal and terrorist activities, those not engaged in crime bear an undue share of the regulatory burden designed to thwart a small fraction of criminal transactions.

Those of us in the Bitcoin space understand the seeming inevitability of what is coming to most monetary systems—a central bank digital currency (CBDC)—as well as its concepts and downsides. If you don't know what a CBDC is, it's vitally important that you learn some of the ramifications of the increasing centralization and digitization of "our" money before it is too late.

Many central banks are discussing the shift from our current digital cash system, where transactions are somewhat private and controlled by individuals, to a system like China's. In this new system, every transaction is fully traceable, controllable, and monitored. This may seem minor to you at first, but it should be sending shivers up the spine of any person who values their autonomy. CBDCs could mean money with an expiration date, restrictions on buying certain things, limits on where you can spend "your" money, and even related social credit scores based on how well you follow the government's rules. These systems of control aren't just futuristic dystopian nightmares; they're already happening in the world's second-largest economy.

Such a system will not be confined to authoritarian or communist regimes. Agustin Carstens, head of the Bank for International Settlements based in Basel, Switzerland, which is the "bank for central banks," recently said that people want "programmable" money. Perhaps programmable money has some useful features. But the big question is, who is the programmer of "your" money? I doubt most people want elected, or especially unelected bureaucrats, in charge of programming what we can do with our money. If a central bank or government are the ones programming it, then it's not really your money!

In a government-controlled and issued fiat monetary system, there will be no choice but to accede to CBDCs to remain in the system. It might seem quite attractive at first. The government will credit money to you, for example, universal basic or Social Security income, via your digital Fed account. At first, advantages will be presented that seem to outweigh the protests of "conspiracy theorists," yet the slope is slippery, and gaining the traction to turn back in the other direction is hard when those in charge dictate the slope.

Contrast this with a decentralized system, not controlled by a single government or entity but rather by a protocol agreed to and maintained by its users. Its ledger is publicly available to all (not just the government) on an immutable blockchain where transactions are transparent, but user information is generally kept opaque by using a private key. There are many great explanations of how this works in the Bitcoin system if you'd like to learn even more. The salient point is the contrast between a centralized system of control and a decentralized system offering individual sovereignty. The ramifications and motives implicit in each are what interests me.

So, given that money is simply a technology for storing, accounting, and transferring the value of individuals' efforts and energy, the relevant question is, "What principles and characteristics serve the creators of value best?" I am not an anarchist or anti-government advocate. Governments can serve the agreed-upon and collective needs of a community. However, value is generated by the energy of the people and, in an ideal and equitable system, contributed to the government as taxes in proportion to the value received by participants. But as governments continually grow their scope and control, we find ourselves to be more the servants of these behemoths than their masters.

19

Me, We, or Us?

We are all connected; To each other, biologically. To the earth, chemically. To the rest of the universe atomically.

—NEIL DEGRASSE TYSON

WE HAVE A CHOICE as to how we view life. We can see it as a "me" proposition. We can see it as about some "we" group, or we can realize the reality that it is an "us." As individualized expressions of life with a unique location in space and time we naturally see the universe through the perspective of our specific positionality. Around that we construct an ego, a personality, a belief structure, and a perspective that defines this me. We can also identify with a group or a community and see ourselves as a we. This is an important identification as it satisfies a human need to belong and be part of a supportive community. Unfortunately, this can result in a view that we are different and better than "they" are and that we must protect ourselves from them. But the reality is, it is an *us* universe. We are all humans living together with millions of other plant and animal species on a little blue dot in space. It takes a shift in perspective to really grasp this.

Edgar Mitchell, an astronaut on the Apollo 14 mission, characterized it this way upon seeing the earth from the perspective of outer space:

> You develop an instant global consciousness, a people orientation, an intense dissatisfaction with the state of the world, and a compulsion to do something about it. From out there on the moon, international politics look so petty.

BALANCE

Life is rarely an all-or-nothing proposition. The point of balance and respect between the individual and the community is a complex affair. How we balance me, we, and us is admittedly not a simple matter, but it is essential. When the scales are tilted too far in one direction or the other (such as beyond what the community has agreed to), it is a recipe for a breakdown. Different individuals and communities with varied participants may make different trade-offs. Someone who chooses to live in a commune will balance different trade-offs and choices than a person who chooses to live alone "off the grid."

How we strike these balances has been the subject of treatises, theories, and postulates for millennia. Yet, when we examine the topics of technology, individuality, and community in the context of monetary systems and Bitcoin, new systems have a greater chance of adoption and success if there is a foundational understanding of the context in which they operate.

In his book, *The Price of Tomorrow*, Jeff Booth issues this call:

> Can we challenge ourselves to create a better system for the world today by, instead of solving for an individual competition, finding a number of bigger goals that we must all solve for the benefit of humanity? A system that, instead of working for narrow parts of our society that pits us against each other, works for the greater "us"? The simple fact is that there is only one human race and all of us belong to it.

There is much debate about the rights of the individual versus the rights of the community. Extremes in any dialogue may demonstrate elements of truth and have validity, but extremes are rarely a basis for collective functioning. Neither anarchy, totalitarianism, nor complete collectivism is likely to strike the right balance for most participants. Those in total control or totally out of control may be attracted to one extreme or another but rarely succeed in bringing long-term value to humanity.

If someone perceives themselves to be a fully sovereign, totally independent, autonomous, and powerful entity, we usually refer to them as having "delusions of grandeur." When someone else perceives themselves as having no value, nothing to contribute, or no life path outside the dictates of a community leader or alleged savior, we might see them as having an immature and underdeveloped understanding of their innate uniqueness and potential.

Hannah Arendt in *The Human Condition* frames the issue this way:

> Their basic error seems to lie in that identification of sovereignty with freedom which has always been taken for granted by political as well as philosophic thought. If it were true that sovereignty and freedom are the same, then indeed no man could be free, because sovereignty, the ideal of uncompromising self-sufficiency and mastership, is contradictory to the very condition of plurality. No man can be sovereign because not one man, but men, inhabit the earth.

Suppose we view individual expression not as a competition between individuals but rather as the manifestation of each person's life energy. In that case, we can respect each unique person within the community of humanity. At the same time, we can also recognize, as Mr. Booth suggests, that we can and should work toward solutions for the greater "us." We don't have to view life through the limiting beliefs that abundance is either for you or for me, or for us or them, but not for everyone. It is not a zero-sum game where what one person does takes away from another. When we are all adding value, it is an additive equation.

THE NETWORK OF CONSCIOUSNESS

Like particles interacting and taking on characteristics of the energetic and positional relationships between other particles in an atom, all living beings (as well as nonsentient matter) are constantly interacting energy fields, taking on traits depending on our positionality, characteristics, and relation with other beings and matter. A human might see a mountain as an inert rock to be climbed or mined. Perhaps the mountain might "see" itself as a force lasting long after a transient bag of skin perishes. All of us impact all that is.

The network effect impacts all technologies and systems. The more widely adopted and dispersed a network is, the greater its impact will be. As networks grow larger, they attract more users—more energy—and become more useful and valuable. Now, what if we step beyond a conventional computer network and look at the largest networks—the universe and consciousness? A network is defined as a group or system of interconnected people or things. The universe meets that definition. And so does consciousness.

Someone might object and say, "Hey, my consciousness is independent, sovereign, and not connected to anything or anyone else." The truth is that while we are each a unique point of consciousness, we are also connected in a network of consciousness. Have you ever been to a sporting event where the crowd's energy took on a collective emotion that you could sense? Take, for example, the collective anxiety at a football/soccer match during overtime, the elation when a player makes a goal seconds before the game-ending buzzer, and the collective despair of the losing team's fans. Thoughts and emotions are transmitted in many other ways, not all as physically direct as we think. Have you ever thought about someone and then "coincidentally" they call you?

And what about when actions result from mass collective thinking that seem unimaginable to an individual? The worst examples are well-known. The German psyche under Hitler had many characteristics of a network effect, wherein people were hooked into a state of consciousness and action that would otherwise be unthinkable. To "drink the Kool-Aid," "go along with the crowd," or "buy into the system" are all phrases we understand to mean being under the influence of a collective state.

Consciousness networks operate at various levels. What might hook one person might not catch another. It is like the frequencies we discussed earlier. Consciousness networks act at various vibrational wavelengths. When we are sitting in a movie theater watching a suspenseful movie, we are all plugged into the field that is being projected to us. At a concert, we are in a different vibrational field. All this is part of a network effect of consciousness.

You might like to think you are acting according to your individual processing of relevant sensory stimuli, but just wait until the person next to you in the theater screams. Perhaps you don't believe in or haven't thought about the network effect of consciousness. What I ask you to consider is, isn't it true, at least to some degree? And if it is, isn't it also possible that it might be true to a much larger degree, even though it just might not (yet) be your experience? The terms "collective consciousness" and "collective unconsciousness" are widely discussed and observed in the fields of psychology, psychiatry, and sociology. The ultimate network just might be the field of consciousness. And the field of consciousness just might be everything.

Albert Einstein put it this way in a 1939 letter:

> A human being is a part of the whole, called by us "Universe," a part limited in time and space. He experiences himself, his thoughts and feelings as something separated from the rest—a kind of optical delusion of his consciousness. This delusion is a kind of prison for us, restricting us to our personal desires and to affection for a few persons nearest to us. Our task must be to free ourselves from this prison by widening our circle of compassion to embrace all living creatures and the whole of nature in its beauty.

Nobody is able to achieve this completely, but the striving for such achievement is in itself a part of the liberation and a foundation for inner security. We should take comfort in knowing that what we perceive as death is merely a transformation, a transition to another form of existence that is beyond our current understanding.

Individual and unique points of energy and consciousness act in relationship to each other. Energy sometimes releases with destructive force (such as the atomic bomb). When energy is in harmony, what may be revealed is the mystery, majesty, and awe of the life force in the form of beauty, love, and the awareness of individuality within unity. That's what we call enlightenment.

20

To Work or Not to Work?

The end of labor is to gain leisure. —**ARISTOTLE**

THROUGHOUT THIS BOOK, I've stressed the importance of proof of work and the creation of true value. But this must not be conflated with the belief that only through "work" is someone valuable or worthy. There is a strong strain in many cultures that only work demonstrates virtue. Historically, that work has often meant hard labor. However, as technology has and will continue to reduce the need for what has traditionally been thought of as "work," we must begin to evolve our understanding of what adding value may look like in the future. Likewise, we will need to develop new structures, modes of thinking, and methods of balancing the distribution of the benefits and responsibilities of the economic and technological developments at the foundation of the new age we are entering.

CAPITALISM AND WORK

Those familiar with Western European, and particularly American culture, understand the concept of the "Protestant ethic" (a term coined by Max Weber in his 1905 book *The Protestant Ethic and the Spirit of Capitalism*). It has its roots in various Protestant denominations, including Puritanism, Calvinism, Lutheranism, and Methodism. This ethic stresses the values of diligence, discipline, frugality, and hard work. Those instilled with this ethic may only see themselves as valuable when working and being "productive." I know I have suffered from this affliction! Virtuous are those who have a "strong work ethic." In short, work is good, idleness is bad. Weber references many sayings of Benjamin Franklin, which became hallmarks of this ethic, such as:

> Remember, that time is money. He that can earn ten shillings a day by his labor, and goes abroad, or sits idle, one half of that day, though he spends but sixpence during his diversion or idleness, ought not to reckon that the only expense; he has really spent, rather thrown away, five shillings, besides.

In other words, if you aren't working and making money, you are wasting your time. And any wasted time comes not just at the expense of what was spent during this "idle" time but also in the lost wages one could have earned. Given that Franklin is one of the founding fathers of the United States, is it any wonder Americans are widely understood to have a philosophy that they live to work rather than work to live? Alexis de Tocqueville, in *Democracy in America*, discussed how Americans, in particular, were afflicted with this "disease of work."

Weber, in his book, elaborates on this "peculiar" work ethic that characterizes a society that instills the feeling that work is both a duty and an intrinsic part of one's being.

> And in truth this peculiar idea, so familiar to us today, but in reality so little a matter of course, of one's duty in a calling, is what is most characteristic of the social ethic of capitalistic culture, and is in a sense the fundamental basis of it. It is an obligation which the individual is supposed to feel and does feel towards the content of his professional activity, no matter in what it consists, in particular no matter whether it appears on the surface as a utilization of his personal powers, or only of his material possessions (as capital).
>
> Of course, this conception has not appeared only under capitalistic conditions. On the contrary, we shall later trace its origins back to a time previous to the advent of capitalism. Still less, naturally, do we maintain: that a conscious acceptance of these ethical maxims on the part of the individuals, entrepreneurs, or laborers in modern capitalistic enterprises, is a condition of the further existence of present day capitalism. The capitalistic economy of the present day is an immense cosmos into which the individual is born, and which presents itself to him, at least as an individual, as an unalterable order of things in which he must live. It forces the individual, in so far as he is involved in the system

of market relationships, to conform to capitalistic rules of action. The manufacturer who in the long run acts counter to these norms, will just as inevitably be eliminated from the economic scene as the worker who cannot or will not adapt himself to them will be thrown into the streets without a job.

Thus the capitalism of today, which has come to dominate economic life, educates and selects the economic subjects which it needs through a process of economic survival of the fittest.

It is not so much that capitalism, Calvinism, or commercialism is the primary or sole cause of this ethic. However, what seems fairly obvious is that existing power structures benefit from instilling a work ethic, whether based on religious grounds or otherwise. Donald R. Heiges, in his book *The Christian's Calling* (1984), noted, "The fact remains that this view of vocation, as developed in Puritanism, provided a very convenient rationale for the leaders of the capitalistic enterprise."

The more productive members of a society are, the more wealth is generated. This is positive for society, unless corruption, manipulation, or the threat of violence are used to produce benefits that skew in favor of elite power structures. Slave labor is the most egregious example. Corporate and government entanglement that restricts free enterprise or results in monopolistic entities are abuses of the principles of a free market.

Winston Churchill noted, "The inherent vice of capitalism is the unequal sharing of blessings." As wealth and income gaps widen, more attention must be paid to the value of what is contributed, as well as to the forces and systems that conspire to limit a more equitable (not equal) distribution of the benefits of enhanced productivity and its resulting wealth.

Our educational industrial system has largely replaced the halls of learning and classical liberalism with vocational or technical training (whether to be a mechanical engineer or an automotive mechanic). It's not that these aren't useful, but we lose something when we replace critical thinking skills, literary familiarity, and historical knowledge solely with these other skills. The system is not teaching us how to think but rather how to get a job. And what happens when those jobs are no longer needed because of robots or AI?

Neil Postman, in *Technopoly: The Surrender of Culture to Technology*, provides a meaningful discussion on how our educational system has been influenced by the shift in culture from being based on history and spiritual traditions that imbue life with meaning to one based primarily on technology and technological advances.

> What do we believe education is for? The answers are discouraging and one of them can be inferred from any television commercial urging the young to stay in school. The commercial will either imply or state explicitly that education will help the persevering student to get a good job. And that's it. [What it] suggests is that the United States is not a culture but merely an economy, which is the last refuge of an exhausted philosophy of education.

Thomas Jefferson said, "An informed citizenry is at the heart of a dynamic democracy." A representative democracy is built on an informed citizenry actively and thoughtfully participating in choosing wise leaders to represent us and ensuring that they do. When our education system focuses only on training people to get a job rather than on how to think critically, we chip away at the necessary ingredients for a Jeffersonian dynamic democracy. As mainstream and social media rely more on rage to draw attention, controversy to promote conflict, scandal to feed prurient interests, and falsehoods and flagrant biases to motivate viewers, we have moved to a state even more precipitous than when Al Gore noted, "The 'well-informed citizenry' is in danger of becoming the 'well-amused audience.'"

Whether it would really be a good system or not, there are no philosopher kings, as Plato suggested might be an ideal form of government. Instead, the alternative to democratic republics seems to be authoritarian regimes driven to secure unlimited power and control in both economic and public spheres of life. Collectivist and communist systems have demonstrated the failure of top-down, centrally planned and managed economies where authoritarian leaders or politburos are allegedly able to make better decisions for society than its actual members. Substituting central planners for the market is as bad as central bankers managing interest rates and monetary supplies. The second part of Churchill's statement quoted above is: "The inherent virtue of socialism is the equal sharing of miseries."

But all these isms have replaced real dialogue and debate about how to balance political and economic forces in order to honor the rights of individuals while living in community. Hurling ism labels is a technique to stifle rational debate and dialogue, making no one wiser, more compassionate, more understanding, or better off.

Sovereign individuals acting within the marketplace have a demonstrably better history of making intelligent decisions based on their knowledge, skills, and preferences. While they may not always be right, by bearing the consequences of their decisions, they can learn from them. Thomas Sowell said,

"Capitalism is not an 'ism.' It is closer to being the opposite of an 'ism' because it is simply the freedom of ordinary people to make whatever economic transactions they can mutually agree to." Capitalism has come to take on a pejorative meaning as an evil force. But as Camille Paglia noted, "Capitalism has its weaknesses. But it is capitalism that ended the stranglehold of the hereditary aristocracies, raised the standard of living for most of the world and enabled the emancipation of women."

The *Merriam-Webster Dictionary* defines capitalism as:

> An economic system characterized by private or corporate ownership of capital goods, by investments that are deter-mined by private decision, and by prices, production, and the distribution of goods that are determined mainly by competition in a free market

Capitalism, at its core, is simply the principle that private citizens who contribute should be able to earn the benefits of their efforts in a free market, save what they do not spend to accumulate capital, and invest that in methods of adding even more value. All participants can freely go to the marketplace to compete and make decisions according to their talents, incli-nations, and preferences. That is not an evil system. But what our structure has morphed into—crony capitalism—is. Robert F. Kennedy, Jr. put it this way: "We do not have free market capitalism in America; we have crony capitalism. There is a huge difference between free-market capitalism, which democratizes a country and makes us more efficient and prosperous, and corporate crony capitalism."

CRONY CAPITALISM

Malcolm S. Salter, in an October 22, 2014, working paper for Harvard University's Edmond J. Safra Research Lab titled "Crony Capitalism, American Style: What Are We Talking About Here?" defined crony capitalism as follows:

Stripped to its essential characteristics, crony capitalism conveys a shared point of view—sometimes stretching to collusion—among industries, their regulators, and Congress that results in business-friendly policies and investments that serve private interests at the expense of the public interest. More specifically, crony capitalism is a special type of moneymaking that economists call "rent seeking." Rent seekers pursue privileged advantages that typically show up as targeted exemptions from legislation, advantageous rules by regulatory agencies, direct subsidies, preferential tariffs, tax breaks, preferred access to credit, and protections from prosecution. The ultimate goal of rent seekers is "grabbing a bigger slice of the [economic] pie rather than making the pie bigger."

Crony capitalism is a problem when innovation, economic efficiency, market pricing, and equal access to government decision makers—that is, fairness—are compromised, and when well-placed persons invest their vast fortunes in teams of lawyers, accountants, lobbyists, and political contributions to ensure that the system continues to work on their behalf. Put somewhat differently, crony capitalism is a form of corruption wherein private parties make undue profit from abuse of public authority—benefiting from the public purse by virtue of their group membership and relationships with public office holders, rather than their "individual and universal citizenship." This form of particularism lacks legitimacy in any governance regime claiming to be democratic. It is corrupt because it undermines integrity in the discharge of duty by public officials.

He goes on to say that, although this definition is straightforward, behavior in the real world is rarely so. That said, I leave it to you to see if this definition doesn't resonate with much of what we see and experience in the United States and much of the rest of the world, regardless of how a country's political system is labeled. With a few twists, the essence of the economic and political problems associated with the intrusion of cronyism can be seen worldwide in many socialist or communist systems and authoritarian states as well.

In the United States (and much of Europe), the corporate nation-state with the money trail that winds through business and politics results in neither democracy as a political system nor capitalism nor even a broad-based socialism as an economic system. Instead, the entrenched interests dine at the feeding trough of corporate campaign donations, lobbyist perks, subtle or implicit bribes and favors, and the revolving door of employment between government and corporations. When scientists at the National Health Institute move to jobs in big pharma or are paid royalties by them for their discoveries, is it any wonder we have an explosion of pharmaceutical "solutions" to every health issue? When politicians and military leaders take jobs at defense contractors, is it any wonder why we always seem to find a way to get into a war so we have to buy more munitions? Selling arms to countries worldwide has become a huge industry that promotes defense contractor interests with explicit approval and sanction by governments. If all this is allegedly in the interest of peace and security, it sure doesn't seem to be working!

When the big private banks own shares of the banks in the Federal Reserve system, it doesn't take a genius to figure out that their interests are more aligned with each other than with the general populace. With the development of big-business industrial food manufacturing companies (many of which were formerly owned by tobacco companies), it's little wonder how processed food has led to huge increases in disease and obesity.

Corporations need boundaries and must face the consequences of their actions. The populace can set limits through their government, but the regulatory lines are blurred in a crony capitalist (or socialist) structure. When banks become too big to fail, their actions have no consequences. Exempting pharmaceutical companies from liability and then having the government mandate their products' use is a framework for exploitation and disaster. That is not a free market system, and we are the ones who pay the price. And, as I discussed in the last chapter, when the guiding principles and standards of a culture are eclipsed by a technology-driven society focused solely on information and economic matters, we lose the framework for balancing the diverse needs of society and humanity.

Separation of the corporation and state should be as important as separation of church and state in the American system. Consensus must be found on how to preserve individual rights and limit monopolistic forces and the intertwining of corporations and the state. As technology dramatically changes the landscape of the future, the necessity of developing new structures and a new point of balance in society is of paramount importance.

There is no economic system that would (or should) meet a dictionary definition of a pure capitalist or socialist label. Some cultures may tilt the balance toward more collective measures to provide economic security for their citizens, while others may lean more toward greater autonomy for private citizens to exercise economic decision-making in a free market. Fighting over which is the "right" system is of more dubious value than being "loving resistance fighters" to authoritarianism, corporate cronyism, and controls on people being able to freely choose which system and culture they prefer to contribute to and be a part of wherever they are found.

THE PROSPECTS AND PERILS OF ARTIFICIAL INTELLIGENCE

A growing concern about AI is that its use and ownership by a limited group of solely profit-driven entities (especially in a crony or authoritarian system) could lead to serious consequences. Geoffrey Hinton, a 2024 Nobel Prize winner who has been referred to as the "godfather of AI," expresses both great optimism and great concern about the unknown and unpredictable nature of its development. In a June 2024 interview on CBS's *60 Minutes*, Hinton addressed many issues raised by AI. He says, "Now is the moment to run experiments to understand AI, for governments to impose regulations, and for a world treaty to ban the use of military robots." Whether government regulation would be helpful or only generate more systems of control (which could be exploited) is an open question. Just as with monetary systems, the issue may come down to whether AI systems become centralized and therefore prone to abuse or decentralized and allowed to flourish and evolve in the free market of ideas.

The dramatic rise of labor-saving and productivity-enhancing technologies has raised the quality of life of much of the world but also presents challenges moving forward. As technology and AI make many jobs obsolete for people, we will need to find new paths for both economic sufficiency and personal meaning. When meaning and purpose are found in work that is no longer necessary, something will need to take its place.

When construction equipment replaced the need for hours of manual labor to clear land, drill through rock, and dig holes, it made it possible to construct buildings, roads, and bridges more quickly and cost-effectively, improving everyone's lives. But the ditch diggers had to find new work, either operating the construction equipment or doing something else. As technological improvements continue and AI is developed, many jobs will be affected.

As robots, machines, and AI begin to replace the need for people, there is a tremendous opportunity to free ourselves from the bonds of labor. But when the old work is gone, people will need to find new ways of expressing their life source energy. Hinton noted, "The risks are having a whole class of people who are unemployed and not valued much because what they used to do is now done by machines."

We will need to find new ways to distribute the benefits of these technological improvements. As discussed, these technological improvements should lead to lower prices (deflation), but our inflationary-designed fiat system prevents this.

Jeff Booth, in *The Price of Tomorrow: Why Deflation Is the Key to an Abundant Future*, succinctly summarizes the issue before us:

> Our economic systems were not built for a world driven by technology where prices keep falling. They were built for a pre-technology era when labour and capital were inextricably linked, an era that counted on growth and inflation, an era where we made money from scarcity and inefficiency. That era is over. But we keep on pretending that those economic systems still work.

The question is, what do we want this new system to look like? It is not only a question of improving our monetary technology (e.g., Bitcoin) but of addressing the ramifications of the increasing pace of technological improvements and the exponential changes that are occurring. In a deflationary system where prices are falling because of the benefits of technology, there will be less pressure on those displaced to have to reeducate and reskill to find new high-paying jobs to keep pace in an inflationary system. Instead, with lower prices, higher standards of living can be supported without continually having to increase income levels. However, wealth and social inequity will grow if the benefits accrue to only a handful of big tech companies. A top-heavy and inflationary system will likely lead to more instability and less potential for all of humanity to share the broadscale benefits of technology.

Some have suggested that a way to fill this gap is some form of universal basic income (UBI). That approach involves having the government send people checks so they can meet the basic expenses of food and shelter. However, since the government's approach to increasing benefits is primarily to increase money printing, the impacts of this approach could only make the problem worse if we remain on a fiat standard. It's very tempting for politicians to promise benefits to everyone. After all, very few people vote against their pocketbooks. And if you can stay in power by spending someone else's money, even better. Economist Art Laffer humorously put it this way: "It is not true that Congress spends money like a drunken sailor. Drunken sailors spend their own money. Congress spends our money."

Without structural changes, a UBI scheme may only widen the gap between those subsisting on government checks while adding little value and those growing wealthy by extracting as much as possible from the system. In the end, it might only perpetuate centralized control systems. What is clear is that we face the challenge of how to distribute the benefits of AI and other technological developments so that all of humanity receives them, not just a few corporations with centralized control. Instead, consensus rules and regulations coupled with open source and decentralized protocols may be a better method of ensuring that the proverbial genie is not let out of the bottle before we have systems, structures, and agreements on how to manage these technological developments.

Suppose the inputs to the large language models (LLMs) that run AI are based on respect, compassion, the recognition of individual rights and responsibilities, the interconnected nature of all life, and the ultimate first principle of love. In that case, the outputs of AI will have these as hallmarks and can serve mankind. If, instead, the inputs are primarily based on profit, competition, power, force, dominance, and physical, psychological, economic, and military control, we will create the dystopian future depicted in the most chilling science fiction horror stories.

Many who deeply understand these technologies warn that they can either serve us or control us. How can we expect AI to be better than we are if we don't stop inputting the language of division and strife into the foundations of these LLMs; instead, let us input paradigms of peace and love into them. Otherwise, when they are smarter than we are, the risks for humanity could be catastrophic.

Hinton put it this way:

It may be we look back and see this as a kind of turning point when humanity had to make the decision about whether to develop these things further and what to do to protect themselves if they did. I don't know. I think my main message is there's enormous uncertainty about what's gonna happen next. These things do understand. And because they understand, we need to think hard about what's going to happen next. And we just don't know.

Through a reframing of these issues and a restructuring of our monetary, economic, educational, and societal structures, we have the opportunity to realize Saifedean Ammous's vision, quoted earlier: "It is about what capital accumulation allows humans to achieve, the flourishing and freedom to seek higher meaning in life when their base needs are met and most pressing dangers averted." Then, the real work can begin—truly becoming aware and appreciative of the amazing nature of life and consciousness.

This can be the promise of tomorrow.

21

The Journey From
Information to Wisdom

Knowledge and wisdom, far from being one,
Have oft-times no connection. Knowledge dwells
In heads replete with thoughts of other men;
Wisdom in minds attentive to their own.

—WILLIAM COWPER

WE NOW HAVE ACCESS to an infinite stream of information. At the press of a button, we can be fed almost anything we seek—or whatever someone else wants us to find! Some of the results returned with an online search may contain nuggets and guide-posts of information that can lead us to a greater understanding of ourselves and our universe. Some, perhaps most, clearly do not. Beyond the debates and concerns about how access to data is used, abused, or monetized are deeper matters that have to do with how to distinguish between data/information, real knowledge, and true wisdom.

The singer-songwriter Tom Waits said, "We are buried beneath the weight of information, which is being confused with knowledge; quantity is being confused with abundance and wealth with happiness." Yet, knowledge is also confused with wisdom.

Having information and knowing things may be classified as knowledge, but it is not the same as wisdom. When Facebook knows both our IP address and that we are asking friends for suggestions about which mattress to buy (so it can inflict ads for mattresses on us), that is information, knowledge even, for it to exploit, but not wisdom.

Dan Millman, author of *The Way of the Peaceful Warrior*, described it like this: "Knowledge is not the same as wisdom. Wisdom is the view from the hill; knowledge is the collection of guidebooks." Wisdom is at the intersection of information, knowledge, experience, perspective, and insight. Masters from Buddha and Jesus Christ to Lao Tzu and many others each arrived at this intersection and, from the top of the hill, offered guidance and value to humankind, pointing us to the paths of compassion, understanding, awareness, and love. These are the enduring wisdom paths anyone can explore and act from.

EVOLUTIONARY KNOWLEDGE

Information and knowledge also have a lot to do with who is using the information and teachings. With a limited perspective, one's ability to truly understand the depth of wisdom shared by these master teachers is also limited. If we choose to go on this journey, the path to knowledge and understanding is an evolutionary one. If we remain stagnant and complacent, the information we encounter will both limit and be limited by our preparedness to grow into possessing a true state of wisdom. As modern physics has revealed, the presence of the observer influences what is observed. The knower and the known are inextricably linked. A third grader's understanding of math will be vastly different from that of a PhD in mathematics who understands differential calculus.

In his book *18 Insights on Life*, Anand Mehrotra shares his perspective on the intersection of knowledge and the knower:

> It is important to realize that knowledge is relevant in proportion to the relevance of the knower and if the knower does not evolve, the knowledge is not evolutionary. It's just information and that information can be used in all kinds of destructive, manipulative ways. So, the knower has to evolve for the knowledge to evolve. As the knower goes through the shift, the knowing goes through the shift too. The potential of the knowledge remains unrealized if one does not evolve. If the knower does not evolve, then they are bound to misunderstand, misappropriate and misuse the knowledge... Knowledge is endless and so too is ignorance; there is no end to misunderstanding.

Growing and evolving in our understanding is an age-old process of mankind, one available to all but engaged in by few. What has been shared by spiritual masters, ancient mythology, and the great books of wisdom shows the way to going beyond the mundane and the inputs of our five senses to the expansion of awareness. To truly become wise, the knowledge must be absorbed and incorporated by a being capable of penetrating beyond the superficial to the depths of ultimate reality. If not, then knowledge is like a seed falling on fallow ground: it will not grow to its potential. And, worse, ignorance could lead to its being misunderstood, manipulated, and abused.

We can view the journey to knowledge and wisdom as having two paths. One is the rational, logical, scientific approach directed toward understanding through external phenomena. The other is the meditative, intuitive, and mystical path. This path looks inward as well as outward. Both are valid methods that have existed and evolved over the course of human history. At different times and in different cultures, each of these paths has gained predominance. We lose much, however, when we believe that only one path is valid. The best science of the time has often been flatly wrong.

For most of human history, the world view of science was that the earth was the center of the universe. Our senses and perception verified this until new instruments were developed that shattered this belief. While philosophers and mystics had imagined and contemplated a different non-geocentric universe before the telescope, this view was generally dismissed in favor of the dominant social and scientific beliefs of the times. Today, quantum mechanics has revealed a universe that defies the logic and perception of the senses in much the same way the telescope forced us to realize the heliocentric nature of our solar system. This is a universe that looks much like that described by the mystical sciences for millennia. Whether in science, religion, or politics, dogma limits, rather than helps evolve, our knowledge and wisdom.

When we hear the phrase today "the science says…" we should understand this in the context that science and human knowledge is an evolving process. To follow or limit ourselves to the "settled science" is a recipe for ignorance. To do so is to treat science like a religion with a settled dogma of beliefs and approved methods of inquiry. Henri Poincaré, the French mathematician, theoretical physicist, engineer, and philosopher of science said, "It is through science that we prove, but through intuition that we discover." The way then to evolutionary wisdom encompasses both paths and we shortchange ourselves and humanity when we rely only on one avenue of inquiry and dismiss the other. Similarly, when we toss out thousands of years of the development of human wisdom from a myriad of sources and traditions, we lose perspective and risk being swallowed by the arrogance of our ignorance masquerading as the only relevant current information.

THE HERO'S JOURNEY

Joseph Campbell, who examined and dissected the intersection of mythology, human psychology, and consciousness, described the template of the "hero's journey," which is present in the stories and myths of nearly all cultures and civilizations, no matter the geography. The hero receives a call to action, often resisting it at first. Signs propel them forward on the journey, where they are faced with obstacles and demons that thwart their progress. Aided by allies and guides, they overcome these challenges to reach a place of insight and wisdom beyond that of normal mortal humans. Having gained wisdom, insight, and enlightenment, they descend back into the world from the heavenly realms of enlightenment to guide others.

Tales of heroes' journeys are found, Campbell demonstrated, in stories from across all cultures and geographies. There is a striking commonality to these myths. Humanity's search for meaning in the face of the unknowable and uncontrollable forces of nature and the universe is symbolically revealed in the tales of mythological heroes. But in the modern world, we have discarded the ancient stories of humanity and, in doing so, lost something of profound value. Campbell writes:

> The problem of mankind today, therefore, is precisely the opposite to that of men in the comparatively stable periods of those great co-ordinating mythologies which now are known as lies. Then all meaning was in the group, in the great anonymous forms, none in the self-expressive individual; today no meaning is in the group—none in the world: all is in the individual. But there the meaning is absolutely unconscious. One does not know toward what one moves. One does not know by what one is propelled. The lines of communication between the conscious and the unconscious zones of the human psyche have all been cut, and we have been split in two.
>
> The hero-deed to be wrought is not today what it was in the century of Galileo. Where then there was darkness, now there is light; but also, where light was, there now is darkness. The modern hero-deed must be that of questing to bring to light again the lost Atlantis of the coordinated soul.

Embarking on the individual hero's journey to transcend the mundane to reach the plane of the transcendental meaning of life is as relevant today as it has been throughout human history. The journey today is more complicated, though, because the inspiration and symbology of mythic tales that once served as guidance have been discarded in favor of science, rationality, and, as discussed earlier, technology. Though these are critically valuable in certain planes of our existence, science falls short when humans attempt to explore life's deeper meanings. Thus, as Campbell says, our psyche is split in two. The task of the heroes of antiquity is the same faced by those of today: it is to cleave together the two halves of our existence—our physical existence in the world of the ephemeral and our aspiration for understanding the deeper meaning of life—and, having done so, guide the rest of us to do the same.

The cofounder of Apple Inc., Steve Jobs, had the impact he did not because he was such an extraordinary coder but because he heard the call and had the vision to deliver something in a new way. He faced demons along the way, only to return. Prior to passing, he directed that those in attendance (including many leaders in business, technology, politics, and the media) be given a copy of Paramahansa Yogananda's book *Autobiography of a Yogi*. According to Walter Isaacson's biography:

> Jobs first read it as a teenager, then reread it in India, and had read it once a year ever since. In 1974, Jobs traveled to India, seeking some spiritual enlightenment. He had the incredible realization that his intuition was his greatest gift, and he needed to look at the world from the inside out, Benioff [Salesforce Company's CEO] said.

Jobs's intuition, nurtured and fueled by his search for spiritual enlightenment, provided the foundation for him to see with a new perspective and vision. He could then translate that vision into the world of technology and foster the development of products that transformed human activity and made Apple one of the world's most valuable companies.

I hear Tina singing again. What's love (and Bitcoin) got to do with it? Glad you asked.

HEARING THE CALL

From the traditional fiat mindset, it is fair to say that taking a hard look at Bitcoin requires looking at money from the inside out. The true leaders of the Bitcoin community are driven by the "incredible realization" of the potential Bitcoin offers. Whether it is working to assist unbanked communities in Africa, freeing enslavement to the currencies and policies of authoritarian nations, offering value transfer mechanisms to those subject to tremendous inflation and capital controls, or restoring the balance between the rights of the individual versus the community, the Bitcoin community is replete with admirable and wise people who are on the hero's journey.

The calls to action come in many forms. They include insights into the insidious and destructive taxation by inflation and how technology has failed to realize the benefits that should be deflationary and make people's lives easier and less costly. The calls are heard in the outrage over restrictions on human endeavors and constraints on individual rights and freedoms imposed by governments and politicians primarily serving their interests rather than the people's. The calls go on and on.

First, though, the call is heard within. It is the inner voice that tells you to go beyond what you were told is possible and to outgrow the conditioning and domestication of our culture and society. Anand Mehrotra captured it in *18 Insights on Life*: "It is the knower evolving to better understand and gain real wisdom." The evolutionary call is the voice that says, "I need a deeper understanding of myself, my heart, and the meaning of my life." In Shakespeare's *Hamlet*, a father gives his son, who is going off to university, this advice: "This above all: to thine own self be true, And it must follow, as the night the day, Thou canst not then be false to any man."

When one is true to oneself, it is easier to hear the call and then take action. And, the actions one takes will be from a place of truth, not from a place of power-seeking, taking advantage, manipulating others, taking more than one contributes, or withholding the love in one's heart. As Robert Pirsig, in *Zen and the Art of Motorcycle Maintenance: An Inquiry into Values*, phrased it, "The place to improve the world is first in one's own heart and head and hands, and then work outward from there."

Answering the call sometimes means going deep down the rabbit hole and truly understanding and gaining awareness of a system that is hard to perceive from within the box. The insights instilled by Satoshi Nakamoto's Bitcoin white paper and the work that followed from it have led many to herald the call to a new decentralized, immutable ledger as a means of accounting, storing, and transferring the value of humanity's efforts.

TELLING THE TALE

The hero's journey, as described by Campbell, occurs in a series of stages after the hero hears the call. From finding allies and villains to overcoming obstacles, the hero faces many challenges during the journey. When the hero triumphs over a supreme ordeal, he gains his true reward. The hero returns to tell the tale and share the wisdom gained from the experience. It is through these journeys and mythic tales from myriad cultures that humanity is propelled forward to an understanding beyond the mundane aspects of everyday life.

Every new age, every new system, and every new idea result from some journey akin to this. When Bill Moyers interviewed Joseph Campbell in a now legendary series of interviews, he did so at George Lucas's Skywalker Ranch. Lucas's *Star Wars* movie is a classic hero's journey tale. There's an exchange during one episode that captures the essence:

CAMPBELL: You see, this thing up here, this consciousness, thinks it's running the shop. It's a secondary organ; it's a secondary organ of a total human being, and it must not put itself in control. It must submit and serve the humanity of the body.

(Clip from *Star Wars*)

DARTH VADER: Join me, and I will complete your training.

CAMPBELL: When it does put itself in control, you get this Vader, the man who's gone over to the intellectual side.

(Clip from *Star Wars*)

LUKE SKYWALKER: I'll never join you!

DARTH VADER: If you only knew the power of the dark side.

CAMPBELL: He isn't thinking, or living in terms of humanity, he's living in terms of a system. And this is the threat to our lives; we all face it, we all operate in our society in relation to a system. Now, is the system going to eat you up and relieve you of your humanity, or are you going to be able to use the system to human purposes?

MOYERS: Would the hero with a thousand faces help us to answer that question, about how to change the system so that we are not serving it?

CAMPBELL: I don't think it would help you to change the system, but it would help you to live in the system as a human being.

MOYERS: By doing what?

CAMPBELL: Well, like Luke Skywalker, not going over, but resisting its impersonal claims.

MOYERS: But I can hear someone out there in the audience saying, "Well, that's all well and good for the imagination of a George Lucas or for the scholarship of a Joseph Campbell, but that isn't what happens in my life."

CAMPBELL: You bet it does. If the person doesn't listen to the demands of his own spiritual and heart life and insists on a certain program, you're going to have a schizophrenic crack-up. The person has put himself off-center; he has aligned himself with a programmatic life, and it's not the one the body's interested in at all. And the world's full of people who have stopped listening to themselves. In my own life, I've had many opportunities to commit myself to a system and to go with it and to obey its requirements. My life has been that of a maverick; I would not submit.

MOYERS: You really believe that the creative spirit ranges on its own out there, beyond the boundaries?

CAMPBELL: Yes, I do.

MOYERS: Something of the hero in that, I don't mean to suggest that you see yourself as a hero.

CAMPBELL: No, I don't, but I see myself as a maverick.

MOYERS: So perhaps the hero lurks in each one of us, when we don't know it.

CAMPBELL: Well, yes, I mean, our life evokes our character, and you find out more about yourself as you go on. And it's very nice to be able to put yourself in situations that will evoke your higher nature rather than your lower.

My call is to implore us to understand that we are on the cusp of this new age and so have choices to make. We may not be able to change all the systems, but we may be able to change some. And those we do change may lead us further into the light of wisdom rather than plunging us deeper into the darkness of ignorance. We can join Darth Vader on the dark side, or we can listen to the spiritual demands of our hearts. We can become Postman's loving resistance fighters, or we can be complacent and acquiesce to the forces that wish to control and extract value from us.

There is no telling how the journey will turn out, nor all the allies, villains, obstacles, and triumphs that may be found along the way. But, as Campbell says in his book *Pathways to Bliss: Mythology and Personal Transformation*:

What I think is that a good life is one hero journey after another. Over and over again, you are called to the realm of adventure, you are called to new horizons. Each time, there is the same problem: do I dare? And then if you do dare, the dangers are there, and the help also, and the fulfillment or the fiasco. There's always the possibility of a fiasco.

But there's also the possibility of bliss.

May the Force be with us.

22

What is Really at the Base?

So you think that money is the root of all evil. Have you ever asked what is the root of all money?

—AYN RAND

BITCOINERS WHO'VE DONE THEIR HOMEWORK and become educated understand the concepts of base and layered money. Monetary theorists and a few economists understand them also. If you have no idea what this means, don't worry, I'll guide you through these concepts. Let's briefly discuss the concept of layered money before examining the next question, "What is really at the base of money?" Once we do that, we can explore what is really at the base of life. By doing so, we can begin to uncover the true meaning of life and embark on a journey toward finding deeper meaning and true liberation.

MONEY LAYERS

In his book *Layered Money*, Nik Bhatia does a great job explaining that money is layered. For much of recent history, gold and silver were the real money—the base money—and paper notes, bills, and debt instruments were layered on top of the base money primarily as technologies of convenience. It was inconvenient and unsafe to transport and settle transactions in physical gold, so paper notes convertible into gold were used. Similarly, intermediaries used ledgers to keep track of transactions so that debits and credits could be offset among numerous parties, thus minimizing the need for the final settlement of every transaction.

In her book *Broken Money*, Lyn Alden also explains these concepts and how new forms of "money" were the result of better technologies being developed to keep pace with the volume and global nature of trade. Gold served as a great "base money" but a poor technology for settlement, so other layers of money were developed to facilitate an increasingly complex world of financial transactions.

This concept is extremely important in understanding monetary systems and how the fiat system replaced gold as base money with paper issued by governments not backed by base money. The fiat currency itself has become the base money.

Yet, whatever system we use, what is at the base of "base money?" As I've asserted and explained throughout this book, money is important for the energy it represents. That energy is the true base of base money in whatever form. Let's use an analogy.

Email beat out physical mail as a faster, more convenient, and more reliable way to communicate. While physical mail still exists and is used, the volume of communication via email versus letters is exponentially greater. Email is a great technology and a very useful base communication format. Yet, it is not the email technology that is fundamental; it is the messages and information we wish to transmit. Again, the map is not the territory, and the letter or the email is not the message. When Marshall McLuhan said, "The medium is the message," he captured the idea that how we transmit something can actually become the message. But when we conflate money with its true message, the impacts are devastating.

A hundred-dollar bill is not the message; it is the transmission mechanism or email of the energy behind it. True money—money with integrity—represents the actual expenditure of energy. Whether physical, intellectual, or creative, it is this effort and value that is important. The work is the message and the origin of the signal. Money is the means of recording such effort and its results—which others find valuable—and using it to trade goods and services.

CONSCIOUSNESS IS THE BASE

As we have discussed, underlying all work, and therefore all money, is energy. We can call that energy by many names. We can be materialists and call it solely the "physical" energy of the cosmos, or we can go deeper and call it consciousness. Consciousness, whatever source you want to attribute it to, clearly exists. Consciousness directs our use of energy in various ways. For some, it drives them to farm and raise food, for others to engineer buildings and bridges, and for others to create literature, music, or art. Without consciousness, we could not direct our energy into work that others find valuable. And without that, there would be no need or use for money.

At the very least, then, the base of money is consciousness. Consciousness is clearly present in human beings. All other sentient beings, while perhaps not to the degree of humans, are also conscious. All life miraculously transforms "food" into their own unique form in an amazing and integrated play of minerals, vitamins, proteins, carbohydrates, fats, and water. These chemicals might seem "inert" yet they transform into the bodily vehicle of life and consciousness as we experience them. If you stop breathing, drinking water, or eating, your consciousness, as you are aware of it in your body, will cease. Consciousness, however, transcends the body.

You can come at it from quantum physics, the systems view of life, or a spiritual perspective, but underneath it all, there is some interconnected field from which all things arise. What that field is is not something we can perceive with our outer five senses or even intellectually easily conceive of. Although having a direct experience and awareness of this underlying presence is not something we sense in day-to-day life, at times, we have probably all had some level of awareness of something much greater than ourselves. The masters, mystics, and spiritual leaders have all taught from this awareness and understanding.

Understanding and awareness of the field of consciousness are critical because, without them, base systems of money can become distorted and manipulated away from the true foundation of life. Just as we can become restricted by the confines of a distorted monetary system, our lives can be limited from achieving our full potential when we do not embrace the path to personal freedom and deeper meaning.

FREEDOM MONEY

Bitcoin is often referred to as freedom money. To many, it represents the possibility of freedom from oppressive governments that control, restrict, or seize the funds of people and organizations that the authorities do not favor.

Many human rights organizations use Bitcoin to transfer funds outside of traditional banking channels that would otherwise be subject to government confiscation. For example, the Anti-Corruption Foundation, affiliated with the late Russian politician and outspoken critic of the current Russian government Alexei Navalny, has used Bitcoin to receive donations and transfer money to supporters in Russia. The organization has had bank accounts in Russia frozen or depleted, so Bitcoin has been the only way to skirt the Russian government's financial repression.

Citizens and organizations in many other countries across the political landscape use Bitcoin because traditional banking systems are not available to them. In his book *Check Your Financial Privilege*, Alex Gladstein outlines numerous examples, from Africa to Cuba to Palestine, where people are using Bitcoin to conduct everyday transactions that would otherwise be impossible due to lack of access to viable financial systems.

Others view Bitcoin as a way to distance themselves from oppressive and extractive banking organizations and financial regulation. Most banks require extensive documentation to open accounts and can place limitations on transactions. It is not uncommon now to be asked the purpose of a transaction when trying to move funds or withdraw any significant sum of cash. If it is your money, why is it any of their business what you are doing with it?

Citizens of many countries are restricted from opening

accounts in other countries even if they are residents there. And this isn't something that applies just to "terrorists" or those from countries labeled as unfriendly. Many foreign banks will not serve American citizens trying to open accounts in their countries because of the extensive reporting and regulatory requirements imposed by the United States. Every US citizen with a financial account outside of the country must report the account and its balance every year to US authorities. In the name of preventing criminal activity, regular law-abiding people are subject to the dragnet of the United States' financial criminal system.

Others see Bitcoin as a pathway to preserve their savings from the persistent inflation of fiat currencies. Bitcoin offers the opportunity to hold money in a system outside the consistently declining value of fiat currencies. Many consider Bitcoin a means to reclaim control over their financial lives, as it frees them from reliance on traditional banking and payment systems. When you can transfer money anywhere in the world to anyone else without getting the approval of gatekeepers or paying excessive fees, that is financial freedom.

As crucial as Bitcoin is as freedom money *from* these things, even more critical is what Bitcoin allows us the freedom *to* do. When we are free from these encumbrances, we can move toward humankind's ultimate freedom. As extractive activities no longer become the focus of attention and as the ability of governments to dilute the value of our efforts through monetary inflation is eliminated, we have the potential to reap both a peace and an economic dividend. There is no simple path to economic sufficiency for all, yet the technological advances we have made provide a huge opportunity to reduce the need for traditional labor while also decreasing prices. If we can also reduce the squandering of resources on endless wars and conflicts, all this energy can be redirected to help humanity flourish.

As we build a stronger foundation of economic security, we have the basis upon which we can explore the deeper meaning of life. This is the opportunity that systems and structures built on the protocol of love and the Bitcoin standard afford us. I won't pretend this will be easy, but bold visions drive humanity toward great things. Do we really want to dream something less?

Bitcoin is a beacon of hope, offering liberation from burdensome, oppressive, and restrictive financial systems. It is the first step toward securing our economic freedom. Bitcoin provides the freedom to break out from the shackles of the fiat system. As we've discussed, this system drains our life energy through inflation, fuels perpetual wars, and curtails individuals' human right to manage their lives and affairs. Bitcoin paves the way for us, as individuals and as a collective, to explore the full potential of our humanity.

As I've argued in this book, Bitcoin has the potential to become a cornerstone of a society that respects and promotes value creation, not extraction. It can help us reclaim our human rights from encroaching government control. And if we operate on the principles of love, an entirely new society can be envisioned. In such a society, we can be free to express and explore our individual and collective humanity. When we break free from social structures that stifle our exploration of life's meaning and our role in expressing our life energy, we can genuinely follow the path to true liberation.

LIFE FORCE

Life force energy flows through all living things. Have you ever observed a shrub cut down to a stump that sends up fresh green shoots and grows anew? This is the life force energy from which we all spring. I don't care what you want to call it, but it is there.

Implicit in this life force energy, when expressed in living beings, is the cycle of birth and death. Every birth in the physical world leads to death. It is part of the bargain of life. Yet, beyond the birth and death of an individual life force, consciousness and the universe continue. Our normal state of consciousness is very connected to our physical bodies. Yet, regardless of what you believe happens after the death of the body, life force energy and consciousness on the planet and in the universe continue. Whether you are an adherent of a religion or spiritual tradition or a quantum physicist, you understand that life, the universe, and consciousness are much greater than any individual being.

In the same way that gold once backed paper bills, it is life force, energy, consciousness, God, or whatever you want to call it, that is the base of life. Thus, it is that energy that is also at the base of any system where humans interact and use the technology of money to account for, store, or transfer our productive channeling of this energy. You can plot routes all day on Google Maps, but that's not the same as actually traveling. You can create or move digital units of money around all day, but they are not the same as their actual energy or value. At the base of money is human consciousness, exploring life, love, and the universe and trying to make sense of it all.

When this life energy materializes as a human being, a house, or a dog, this creation will eventually experience decay and death. And from this death comes the stuff of a new birth. In the next section, we'll take a closer look at this cycle and how life and the cycles of history intersect to provide new opportunities and new life to humanity and society. But before we do that, let's discuss the ultimate question.

THE MEANING OF LIFE

I'm sorry, but I don't have a simple, universal answer for you. But we can all go deep and explore the meaning of our individual lives within this network of life and consciousness. How each life expresses itself and its search for meaning is different. The state of our consciousness, what we value, and whether or not we are willing to take evolutionary action will frame our journey. Yet, the final destination is the same. Abraham Maslow placed it at the top of his hierarchy of human needs and called it "self-actualization."

Someone wiser than I am, Anand Mehrotra, in his book *18 Insights on Life*, explains this journey and its requirements as the following:

> The whole of human life is in search of meaning and that meaning is a reflection of the state of consciousness, how they flow within the relative reality. Every individual has an idea of what they want in their life, a certain meaning to which they are devoted. Everyone is looking for their own version of sacred nature, for greatness within themselves. Our whole being is designed to evolve, our brains designed to learn. We are capable of phenomenal creativity. Our bodies are capable of generating incredible, transcendental experiences. We are all looking in our own way, trying to find happiness, trying to find meaning, trying to find a certain sense of self-worth. Everyone is looking, whether they are looking in a correct manner or an incorrect manner; whatever their nature is, that is what they will find. We choose the direction in which we flow. If we look to be influenced by cultural icons and celebrities, these will be our deities and cultural archetypes.

To be noble is to be a soul realising its nature, gaining that nobility, moving in the direction of cosmic consciousness, not being born into nobility. So those who start to move in the direction of knowledge, looking for self-realisation, the true spirit, move towards liberation.

The confines of our minds, our belief systems, and our societal structures can support or detract from this journey. We will all be better served if we free ourselves from limiting beliefs about what is possible and what is not. We stand on the cusp of a new age with great potential to support us all in our shared quest for liberation. When we as individuals do our own work and then, as part of society, come together to construct and embrace systems to support us all on this journey, that period between birth and death in these bodies will have deep meaning.

23

Birth, Death, and Money

There is no cure for birth and death save to enjoy the interval.
—GEORGE SANTAYANA

IN HIS SEMINAL WORK, *The Hero with a Thousand Faces*, Joseph Campbell cites Arnold Toynbee's work on the rise and disintegration of civilizations.

> Schism in the soul, schism in the body social, will not be resolved by any scheme of return to the good old days

(archaism), or by programs guaranteed to render an ideal projected future (futurism), or even by the most realistic, hardheaded work to weld together again the deteriorating elements. Only birth can conquer death—by birth, not of the old thing again, but of something new. Within the soul, within the body social, there must be—if we are to experience long survival—a continuous "recurrence of birth" to nullify the unremitting recurrences of death.

HISTORY'S CYCLES

Those familiar with William Strauss and Neil Howe's book *The Fourth Turning* will recognize the concept that history has a cyclical element, like the four seasons, rather than being just a linear progression. There is the birth of the new in the spring, full blossoming in the summer, decay and leaves dropping in the autumn, and clearing away in the winter. This clearing away paves the way for new birth in the spring.

Strauss and Howe demonstrate that this cyclicality also applies to changes in the attitudes and behaviors of different generations. These characteristics are then reflected in social and governmental structures. A cycle lasts about the length of a long lifetime and can be divided into four phases, each lasting twenty to twenty-five years.

We can appreciate this concept as we observe the distinct differences between recent generations. In the United States and much of Western Europe, we have the WWII, so-called Greatest Generation, then the lost generation, boomers, Gen X, millennials, and Gen Z. Each group has unique characteristics shaped by their place in the historical cycle, and each responds to the needs of their time differently.

In his latest work, *The Fourth Turning Is Here*, Howe posits that Western societies are currently in the last phase—the winter or fourth turning of a societal cycle. Fourth turnings are characterized by the decline in confidence in the old structures, societal dissension as structures break down, and conflicts over what the new systems should look like. Unfortunately, fourth turnings have been characterized by a dramatic and traumatic clearing out of the old, frequently through war.

As all this suggests, it is worth considering that the birth of new systems will come after the decline and clearing away of the old ones. Death follows birth as surely as birth follows death. We can limit our analysis of money to purely economic and monetarist contexts, but much may be gained when we consider money and monetary systems in a broader setting.

In the yogic teachings, the godhead has three aspects: Brahma, the creator; Vishnu, the sustainer; and Shiva, the destroyer. All three are intrinsic parts of each other and of the cycle of life. Things are created, maintained for a period, and then destroyed, and the cycle repeats.

When we are in a cycle that was birthed before we were, and the system is in maintenance mode, it is difficult to perceive this cycle without expanding our perspective. A myopic view leads us to think that how things are is just how they are and that this is right, normal, and will continue. Like an eighteen-year-old who cannot conceive that death lies ahead of them, it is hard for people living under fiat systems to see the possibility of the death of those systems and to imagine the birth of something new. What that new thing or system is or will be is uncertain, but what is certain is that the old will be cleared away, and something new will be born.

END OF THE OLD, BIRTH OF THE NEW

Is this Bitcoin? Has the new system already arrived? Only time will tell. For now, let's admit that all the signs that the old system is in decline are coming into view. Massive government, business, and personal debt, fundamental distrust in political and governmental systems, and social unrest are the hallmarks of a historical cycle's winter. For true believers in Bitcoin's potential to pave the way for a new economic and monetary system, we see it as a new birth as the old system begins its death rattle.

Many see Bitcoin and, ugh, crypto as just some way to make a quick buck within the framework of the current system. As a result, in the world of other "cryptocurrencies," we get all the faults of the old system without the benefits of a new paradigm. We find initial coin offerings without disclosures or demonstrable benefits, excessive leverage, pump-and-dump schemes, and more. These schemes are all characteristic of the dying system.

As a technology, Bitcoin demonstrates many advantages over existing fiat monetary systems. It addresses flaws in the fiat system, such as governments' ability to create more money, act in a manner the populace might not support, and sprinkle largesse and political favors to retain power. With a protocol that precludes monetary expansion beyond the programmed twenty-one million Bitcoins, these flaws are diminished. Adoption of a Bitcoin standard would limit the ability of governments to use money for political and military aggrandizement beyond the support of the people. Under a fiat system, governments are not subject to monetary restraint. The Bitcoin protocols have tremendous potential for limiting self-serving governmental actions.

Whether old or new to the Bitcoin community, the onus is on those of us who see the benefits of this new path to continue to educate others and, in our words and actions, demonstrate the appeal and worthiness of the core values of the Bitcoin ethos. The opportunity and challenge is to attract others to this new system, not just to criticize the old and cheer its burning.

Dislocations and pain are inherent in substantial change. Spring does not come without the freeze of winter. There will be those who mock it when the warmth of the new system is offered to them. In such cases, they may find themselves shut out in the cold because they couldn't see winter coming. But if a new global monetary system is to succeed, everyone must be invited, encouraged, and welcomed whenever they arrive. Of course, as the saying goes, everyone will get Bitcoin at the price they deserve. Some—those who understood it when Bitcoin was in its infancy—sit by a fire of great wealth. Others who are newer are only beginning to feel the warmth. Bitcoin is still a relatively small asset class. Don't underestimate how early we are in this system and how much more room there is for the network to grow and for wealth in Bitcoin to accumulate.

It is just an inherent fact of new systems that those who embrace and adopt them earlier will have certain advantages as the system expands. Just as when the automobile industry began, there will be challenges at first. Back then, as some people embraced the adoption of autos, others tried to protect the horse and buggy industry. The people who opened gas stations first benefited, while others who failed to adapt, like those who manufactured horse carriages, struggled, fought the change, and eventually were cleared away.

It is precious and sacred to witness a new birth and observe, guide, and participate in the growth of a new being. The life force that brings forth a new baby is beyond our understanding or comprehension. We can understand its mechanics, but we must stand in awe of the mystery and majesty of life. A new life is the result of an astronomical number of possibilities, potentialities, and actualities that had to occur for a particular baby to be born. While a new being is a unique individual expression of life, it did not manifest just because of its parents' actions. All life is the product of everything that preceded it.

Bitcoin is a new money. While it is often said it had an "immaculate conception," this describes its ethical foundation, not its technology or utility. Bitcoin, as a new life, was built on the shoulders of the efforts of the people who preceded it—the growth of monetary systems from shells to gold to fiat, the harnessing of electricity and the development of silicon chips, and the evolution of complex mathematics and cryptography. Its ultimate value and utility will depend on how all of humanity uses it in the future.

As Toynbee and history itself show, grand schemes built on top of deteriorating old systems are likely to fail. Something new must be born to transcend the death of the old. As the first engineered digital money to be created, Bitcoin is clearly brand-new. Whether it will thrive, grow to maturity and old age before dying, or be transformed into something else remains to be seen. Bitcoin offers a near-limitless capacity to store and transfer the energy and value of human activity without dilution from governmental or political forces. The choice is between hitching your future to the past or nurturing the birth of the promising new. Gold reigned as money for thousands of years. A vastly superior technology has the potential to reign for even longer.

If we survey the landscape, there are many signs that we are on the cusp of a period when old systems and patterns are being destroyed and new paradigms are being birthed. The pace, breadth, and scope of technological innovation alone heralds dramatic changes in our individual and collective lives. Technology holds the promise of significantly expanding our lives, the efficiency of our efforts, and our spheres of understanding and influence. Information, ideas, and communication are globally accessible in ways undreamed of only a few decades ago.

Yet, technology is merely a tool for humanity's aspirations. The nature of these aspirations can guide the birth of new systems, societies, and relationships, aided by how we view and use technology's potential. It will take vision, foresight, and collective will to embrace a future that is less dystopian and more utopian than the one we may be facing.

24

Dream On

*You know you're in love when you can't fall asleep because
reality is finally better than your dreams.*

—DR. SEUSS

WE ALL HAVE DREAMS, literal and figurative. We daydream, and
we nightdream. Dreams are important ways for us to envision
possibilities and let our imaginations run wild with the sparks
of inspiration we receive. At times, our literal dreams at night
bring glimpses of other worlds, connections, and relationships.

ENVISIONING

According to Don Miguel Ruiz, who popularized the Toltec tradition of Mexico in his book *The Four Agreements*, the Toltec philosophy takes the concept of dreams a bit further. In this tradition, dreams are said to be the way we assemble our vision of reality. We "dream" the way we see the world.

Unfortunately, many people's "dreams," or their visions of the world, are full of fear, danger, hatred, anger, jealousy, and trauma. It is hard to be joyful if your vision of reality is harsh and judgmental. On the other hand, some see beauty, abundance, magnificence, joy, and love as their primary vision of reality. While they may face and acknowledge challenges, their fundamental dreams are of a world of possibilities, connection, and love.

Many spiritual and psychological traditions hold that, depending on how you perceive reality, this life is either heaven or hell. One type of dream holds a vision of heaven on earth; the other is a dream of hell. If you view this world as merely a stepping stone to some distant future heaven, it tends to be easier to accept hell on earth rather than to create heaven here and now.

COLLECTIVE DREAMING

In the Toltec tradition, it is not only individual dreams that matter but also the collective's dream. Don Miguel Ruiz calls this the "dream of the planet." Together, individual dreams or nightmares form a state of consciousness for society. We are all born into families, cultures, and societies that have their own dreams. We become conditioned and, in his phrase, "domesticated" by the people we are surrounded by, depend on, and learn from. We are taught who and what we are, what the right way to behave is, and how to get rewarded for complying with the demands of our parents, teachers, and communities. We are good boys and girls if we do as we are told and bad if we do not. Our dreams take on the characteristics and possibilities of the dream states or consciousness of those around us.

We are told what we are—smart, dumb; or this religion, nationality, or race; part of this group or tribe; a fan of this team; and so on and so on. If we enter the world as mainly a blank canvas, it gets filled in for us before we can even pick up a paintbrush! When we restrict ourselves to the beliefs placed on us, we limit our dreams. And if these beliefs put us in a living hell on earth, it takes a mighty sword to slay that dragon.

These dreams created for and by us, however, the Toltecs say, are *mitote*, not reality. As Don Miguel Ruiz describes, it is as if we are looking into a smoky mirror, the reflection hazy and distorted. In the East, they call this maya, the world of illusions. It is not that it is not real, but it is not reality either. This is much like the way quantum physics shows us that while our perception that objects are solid is real, their underlying reality is the movement and vibration of energy particles within a vast void.

Oh boy, I hear Tina singing again. Hold on, I'll get there.

TOLTEC TALENT SHOW

My wife, Denise, spent a long time studying and teaching Toltec wisdom as one of the few teachers certified to teach it by Don Miguel Ruiz. So, as part of our building a new dream, we went on a journey to Teotihuacán, an ancient city and pyramid complex outside Mexico City, to explore Toltec practices.

At the end of our weeklong journey, the leader of the quest

had us all participate in a talent show. Now, frankly, I thought it was a pretty silly idea. Perhaps that's because I feel relatively talentless when it comes to performance of any kind. But before long, I ended up as the emcee. It was an energy-filled, hilarious, and joyful evening. But still, I had to come up with some kind of act, not just introduce everyone else. While I dabbled in playing piano, clarinet, and guitar in my youth, there was one standout instrument for me—the air guitar.

The week of dream journeys we'd had was behind us, and as the performance evening was drawing to a close, I cued up Aerosmith's "Dream On," pressed play, and launched into an air guitar solo, bringing in other guys as air rhythm guitars and an air drum section to jam. Then, in a highlight moment, my beloved fell to her knees as my biggest groupie fan.

Dream, dream, dream until your dreams come true.

CHOOSING THE DREAM

You see, we have the choice to dream the dream we want to dream. When the dream of the planet is of scarcity, violence, greed, force, dominance, and selfishness, this angst-inducing cacophony will be the soundtrack of our lives. We can live in our own personal hell, or we can live in our own personal heaven, no matter what the circumstances. There is probably no greater testament to this than psychiatrist Viktor Frankl's book *Man's Search for Meaning*. Imprisoned in a Nazi concentration camp, he faced brutality and suffering yet chose to look for meaning within the experience. He could not avoid the pain, but he could choose not to suffer. He could not change his circumstances, but he could decide how to cope with them. He could look behind this reality to find deeper meaning and greater spiritual understanding.

It's a pretty big jump from Aerosmith to Viktor Frankl. Now let's jump back to Bitcoin.

THE BITCOIN VISION

Well, the money that energy represents is, in many ways, just a marker for our dreams. If someone dreams of being a musician, practices to learn and develop their skills, and expresses their deepest self through music, the energy of this music may resonate beyond them. They may strike a deeper chord within themselves and others and enter a vibrational field where listeners hear more than just musical notes. They find meaning, harmony, beauty, and even a symphony of life's expression. Now that's something worth devoting your life to!

The governments, politicians, and leaders who strive for power and dominance thrust their dreams on everyone else, thereby limiting the possibility and reality of other dreams. No matter the intentions, the most dangerous humans are the ones who, believing they are right, are convinced they must foist their dreams on others. When one does not have true wisdom and understanding it is easy to travel (or be led down) the wrong path. In the yogic tradition, they call this powerful but destructive force avidya or incorrect knowledge.

I previously discussed the difference between information, knowledge, and wisdom. There are a great many people with access to tremendous information and who seem knowledgeable due to their ability to cite or regurgitate it. Wisdom, however, is coupled with understanding, awareness, and experience. There is also a difference between believing and knowing. We can believe that "life's a bitch and then you die" and dream nightmares, or we can dig deeper, as Viktor Frankl did, for a knowingness of life's greater meaning and purpose.

My intent in this book is to encourage people—both those who are entrenched in the old systems and those who are intrigued by new systems—to dream a dream worthy of the amazing life source energy that we are all part of. We will manifest what we dream. If we focus mostly on tearing down the old or getting rich, our dream will likely be a hazy mirror.

Bitcoin offers a new possibility for reimagining money as a tool with which we can all manifest our individual dreams, respect different visions, and dream a new dream of the planet. We have millennia of great wisdom traditions to guide us. How we dream and what we dream are what we will bring into creation.

As in any hero's journey, we will likely face great trials, upheavals, and challenges as we chart a new course for a new age. The questions for all of us are: What is our dream? What dream do we want to contribute to? And, are we dreaming a dream of the planet that will create heaven or hell on earth?

Dream on.

Afterword

I HOPE THAT, in reading this book, you will be prompted to think more deeply and broadly about how all of society's systems and structures, from money and Bitcoin to education and the arts to technology and government, reflect the values and aspirations of humanity. Every generation, every century, and every epoch brings new challenges and new possibilities. Only by consciously and intentionally reflecting on our values and designing systems that support them will we achieve what is possible. As the Renaissance and then the Enlightenment followed the Dark Ages and ushered in a new chapter in humankind's growth and evolution, so we stand at the cusp of a new digital age.

There are always forces of light and darkness at play, but light will always dissolve the darkness. The opportunity before us is to be the carriers and projectors of light. Since darkness is merely the absence of light, the more we all shine our light, the more darkness will be dissolved. The light we shine must come from our deepest essence as conscious and aware humans. Each of us must nurture our own flame based on authenticity, universal truths, and love. If we do this, what we create can serve all humanity. Martin Luther King, Jr. said, "Darkness cannot drive out darkness; only light can do that. Hate cannot drive out hate; only love can do that."

David R. Hawkins, MD, PhD, in his book *Power vs. Force*, puts it this way:

> Ignorance does not yield to attack, but it dissipates in the light, and nothing dissolves dishonesty faster than the simple act of revealing the truth. The only way to enhance one's power in the world is by increasing one's integrity, understanding, and capacity for compassion. If the diverse populations of mankind can be brought to this realization, the survival of human society and the happiness of its members is secure.

As we enter a new digital epoch, we stand at a precipice with tremendous new opportunities and challenges in front of us. We can develop astounding new technologies, but if their use is not based on universal principles, truth, and service to all humanity, they will be co-opted and corrupted, condemning us to greater darkness.

The Christian faith teaches that "God so loved the world he gave his only son" (John 3:16). The message of that son has persisted, but it has also been distorted at times by intermediaries. Satoshi gave the world Bitcoin and then walked away. But as fallible humans can corrupt any system, even a protocol so immaculately conceived as Bitcoin can fail if not guided by the principle of love.

Many posit that the duality of individual sovereignty and the collective restrains and constrains the free expression of the individual. Each individual expression within that system is as valuable as any other, yet to imagine it as separate and apart is a fallacy. Regardless of whether you come at it from a spiritual perspective or from systems theory, the reality is that we are individual expressions of life within a complex web. We are all points in time and space, unique expressions of life with valuable perspectives. Yet, we are also an integral part and expression of a unified whole. There is singularity within plurality.

Money is deeply woven into every aspect of our modern world. How we build and use (or misuse) monetary systems affects everything we do. If we improve our monetary system, we may get a chance to reshape human and economic dynamics. This can allow each one of us to direct our energy toward nurturing the value we can bring and give us room to explore the deeper meaning of life and its expression in human form.

Creating real systemic change requires that we transform the intentions, thoughts, and perspectives underlying what no longer works; otherwise, the same patterns will repeat.

Robert M. Pirsig, in *Zen and the Art of Motorcycle Maintenance: An Inquiry into Values*, put it this way:

To tear down a factory or to revolt against a government or to avoid repair of a motorcycle because it is a system is to attack effects rather than causes; and as long as the attack is upon effects only, no change is possible. The true system, the real system, is our present construction of systematic thought itself, rationality itself, and if a factory is torn down but the rationality which produced it is left standing, then that rationality will simply produce another factory. If a revolution destroys a systematic government, but the systematic patterns of thought that produced that government are left intact, then those patterns will repeat themselves in the succeeding government. There's so much talk about the system. And so little understanding.

It will take more than Bitcoin or any new monetary system or government structure to change our way of thinking. We must deepen our level of awareness and understanding of the true nature of life and reality to shift out of our patterns and work together in greater harmony.

The opportunity is to ground ourselves, our perspectives, and our expressions in awe, gratitude, respect, and love. Without this, no protocol, process, technology, or society will achieve its potential to consciously recognize and value each and every member while at the same time being aware of our intrinsic and fundamental interconnectedness.

If our foundation is based on these principles, we can create a freer, fairer, and more peaceful world. With a Bitcoin standard based on love, we can fix the money and fix the world.

Acknowledgments

I AM GRATEFUL for so many who have guided me along my life's journey and the path that led me to writing this book. You may not know how you contributed to my growth and evolution (and I might have even resisted it at the time), but I appreciate the myriad of people that I have crossed paths with, both in various professional careers and personally.

When that path quite unexpectedly led me to Bitcoin, I found new sources of great wisdom that allowed me to reexamine my understanding of money, finance, and economics, as well as many aspects of life where I saw problems that I had not connected back to money. Many of these people and resources are listed in the Resources and References section. There are many more I have learned from, whether at conferences or through podcasts or YouTube videos. I am deeply grateful to you all for the groundbreaking work you have done to shine a light on the problems of our current system and on the potential solutions. And, of course, there is Satoshi Nakamoto.

I am deeply appreciative to those who helped me complete and bring this book forward. Marie Timmel worked through two exhaustive rounds of edits to vastly improve the manuscript. Mark Karis brilliantly brought together and harmonized graphically the diverse elements of the book for the cover. Jennie Cohen gave a final polish to the manuscript. Dear friends Alexandra Seigle, Deborah Woodward, and Jürgen Nagler caught what I hope were the last remaining errors that had snuck through. Rodney Hatfield helped me put all the pieces together to get this over the finish line for publishing and reach my audience.

As my journey and this book transcends much more than money and finance, I owe even deeper gratitude to the thought leaders and wisdom teachers who have helped form, guide, and illuminate a more profound understanding of a seemingly incomprehensible vast universe and web of life. From an early age, Fritjof Capra's work brought together the depth and similarity of scientific knowledge from modern quantum physics and the mystical sciences of Eastern wisdom traditions. After I'd drifted for many years, Anand Mehrotra in India helped me reconnect all the dots to a knowingness beyond information and theory. There are many other wise masters from varied traditions and the sciences (again, some of whom are listed in the "Resources and References" section) who have guided me along the ultimate journey in life—that of a greater understanding of who and what I truly am.

As one of the objectives of this book is to help answer the question, what's love got to do with it? my deepest gratitude is to those who have shown me, in a very personal way, what love is. It is an honor and privilege to facilitate the entry into this world of my two children, Mitch and Grace. I have done my best (though at times undoubtedly fallen short) in trying to guide as well as learn from you. Lastly is my phoenixlike wife, Denise, upon whose wings I have journeyed through my own path of resurrection, renewal, and rebirth. My deepest desire is that I do my best to love, support, and honor you on your own unique journey.

About the Author

PAUL ROGERS spent twenty years in financial planning and investment management in the United States. He was a Certified Financial Planner ®, worked for a large national brokerage firm, and owned his own independent practice. Previously, he worked in civil rights enforcement and environmental protection with federal and state agencies. A philosophy major, his passion has always been a deeper understanding of life. After leaving the world of traditional finance, where he thoroughly dismissed Bitcoin, he went to India for yoga training just as the global pandemic broke. Returning, he had an aha moment, which led him to emerge from the finance world's cave of shadows into the light and embrace the new monetary technology of Bitcoin. His passion is to help people understand what money represents and how distorted messages can influence and corrupt our systems and values. By weaving together money, Bitcoin, quantum physics, Eastern and other wisdom traditions, history, technology, the twin concepts of sovereignty and community, sex, love, birth, and death into a more coherent framework, he hopes to inspire a vision for creating and experiencing a freer, fairer, more peaceful and loving world.

Resources and References

Alden, Lyn, "Bitcoin's Energy Usage Isn't a Problem. Here's Why." *Strategic Investment Newsletter*, August 2021, updated January 2023.

Alden, Lyn, *Broken Money: Why Our Financial System Is Failing Us and How We Can Make It Better*. Timestamp Press, 2023.

Ammous, Saifedean, *The Bitcoin Standard*. Wiley, 2018.

Ammous, Saifedean, *The Fiat Standard: The Debt Slavery Alternative to Human Civilization*. Saif House, 2021.

Arendt, Hannah, *The Human Condition*. University of Chicago Press, 1958.

Bhatia, Nikhil, *Layered Money: From Gold and Dollars to Bitcoin and Central Bank Digital Currencies*. Nikhil Bhatia, 2021.

Booth, Jeff, *The Price of Tomorrow: Why Deflation Is the Key to an Abundant Future*. Stanley Press, 2020.

Broughel, James, "Custodia Bank Case Highlights Federal Reserve Hypocrisy Toward Crypto." *Forbes*, April 25, 2023.

Cambell, Joseph, *The Hero with a Thousand Faces* (The Collected Works of Joseph Campbell). Joseph Campbell Foundation, 2020.

Cambell, Joseph, *Pathways to Bliss: Mythology and Personal Transformation* (The Collected Works of Joseph Campbell). Joseph Campbell Foundation, 2018.

Capra, Fritjof, *The Tao of Physics*. Shambhala, 2010.

Capra, Fritjof, and Pier Luigi Luisi, *The Systems View of Life: A Unifying Vision*. Cambridge University Press, 2014.

Carter, Nic, "How Much Energy Does Bitcoin Actually Consume?" *Harvard Business Review*, 2021.

Dalai Lama XIV, *The Art of Happiness*. Riverhead Books, 2009.

Dalai Lama XIV, *Toward a True Kinship of Faiths: How the World's Religions Can Come Together*. Harmony, 2010.

Farrington, Allen, and Sacha Meyers, *Bitcoin Is Venice: Essays on the Past and Future of Capitalism*. BTC Media Inc., 2022.

Frankl, Viktor, *Man's Search for Meaning.* Beacon Press, 2006.

Gladstein, Alex, *Check your Financial Privilege.* BTC Media, LLC, 2022.

Gladstein, Alex, "The Invisible Cost of War in the Age of Quantitative Easing." *Bitcoin Magazine*, March 2, 2022.

Hawkins, David R., *Power vs. Force, The Hidden Determinants of Human Behavior.* Hay House Inc., 1995.

Hayek, F. A., *The Road to Serfdom, The Definitive Edition.* University of Chicago Press reprint, 2007.

Heiges, Donald R, *The Christian's Calling.* Fortress Press, 1984.

Howe, Neil, *The Fourth Turning Is Here: What the Seasons of History Tell Us About How and When This Crisis Will End.* Simon & Schuster, 2023.

Issacson, Walter, *Steve Jobs.* Simon & Schuster, 2011.

Khalil, Abubakar Nur, "Africans Are Pioneering the Bright, Yet Complicated, Green Future of Bitcoin Mining." *Forbes,* May 24, 2024.

Lipton, Bruce, *The Biology of Belief: Unleashing the Power of Consciousness, Matter, and Miracles.* Hay House Inc., 2015.

Long, Barry, *Making Love the Divine Way.* Barry Long Books, 2014.

Lyman, Sam, "Why Bitcoin Mining Might Actually Be Great for Sustainability." *Forbes*, September 21, 2023.

McDonald, Chris, *How Institutional Buyers Are Changing the Face of the U.S. Housing Market.* Yahoo!Finance, November 3, 2023.

Mehrotra, Anand, *18 Insights on Life: For Contemporary Times from the Gita.* Notion Press, 2023.

Mehrotra, Anand, *Liberation: An Interpretation of Isha Upanishad.* Sattva Publications Pvt Ltd, 2020.

Millman, Dan, *The Way of The Peaceful Warrior.* H J Kramer, 2000.

Novak, Les, "Harnessing Africa's Energy Transition: Bitcoin Mining as a Catalyst." *Medium*, May 11, 2024.

Perkins, John, *Confessions of an Economic Hitman.* Berrett-Koehler Publishers, 2023.

Postman, Neil, *Technopoly: The Surrender of Culture to Technology.* Vintage, 1993.

Qureshi, Zia, "Rising Inequality: A Major Issue of Our Time." Brookings Institute, May 16, 2023.

Richardson, Diana, *Slow Sex*. Destiny Books, 2011.

Richardson, Diana, *Tantric Orgasm for Women*. Destiny Books, 2004.

Richardson, Diana, and Michael Richardson, *Tantric Sex for Men: Making Love a Meditation*. Destiny Books, 2010.

Rogers, Paul, "Bits of Wisdom: Insights on Money, Our Monetary System, and Bitcoin," ten-part series. YouTube, https://www.youtube.com/channel/UCV2lozppHqtcEmGGpjSFI9A

Rothbard, Murray, *The Case Against the Fed*, Ludwig von Mises Institute, 2007.

Rothbard, Murray, *The Mystery of Banking*. Ludwig von Mises Institute, 2008.

Roy, Arundhati, *War Talk*. South End Press, 2003.

Ruiz, Don Miguel, *The Four Agreements*. Amber-Allen Publishing, 2011.

Ruiz, Don Miguel, *The Mastery of Love*. Amber-Allen Publishing, 2011.

Ruiz, Don Miguel, *The Mastery of Self*. Hierophant Publishing, 2016.

Sadhguru, *Inner Engineering: A Yogi's Guide to Joy.* Harmony, 2016.

Salter, Malcolm S., "Crony Capitalism, American Style: What Are We Talking About Here?" Harvard University, October 22, 2014.

Shahbaz, Adrian, "The Rise of Digital Authoritarianism." Freedom House, 2018.

Strauss, William, and Neil Howe, *The Fourth Turning: What the Cycles of History Tell Us About America's Next Rendezvous with Destiny.* Crown, 2009.

Tobin, Michael, and Ian Birrell, "The African Village Mining Bitcoin." UnHerd, January 5, 2022.

Weber, Axel, *Inflation Not Only Hurts, It Diverts.* Foundation for Economic Education, February 9, 2023.

Weber, Max, *The Protestant Ethic and the Spirit of Capitalism.* Penguin Classics, 2002.

Yogananda, Paramahansa, *Autobiography of a Yogi.* Self-Realization Fellowship, 1998.